Behind the Story

Stories, personal anecdotes and reflections from the journal of Wycliffe author,

HUGH STEVEN

CREDO
PUBLISHING CORPORATION

Published by CREDO Publishing Corporation
All Rights Reserved

ISBN 0-920479-14-6
(paperback)

Cover art work by Dale Cooper

CREDO Publishing Corporation
#103, 19623-56 Avenue
Langley, B.C.
V3A 3X7

Printed in the United States of America

ACKNOWLEDGEMENTS

The formulation and development of my early biblical philosophy I owe to men whom I met only through their writing. Two names stand out above all the rest—C.S. Lewis and J.B. Phillips. Thus it was a singular joy to receive a personal letter from Mrs. Vera Phillips, wife of the late J.B. Phillips, granting me permission to quote from her husband's book, *The Newborn Christian*.[1]

I wish to acknowledge that the story "Wound for Wound" and "Bridge of Pain" originally appeared in *Power for Living*, a Scripture Press Publication. The two chapters, "I'm Losing my Job and I'm Happy" and "Data Incomplete" appeared originally in *Young Ambassador*, a publication of the Good News Broadcasting Association, Inc. Book rights retained.

A special word of appreciation should be given to several SIL Branches and Divisions along with their directors and staff, especially Dick Hugoniot of the Indonesian Branch and Bob Whitesides of the Central America Branch, who graciously provided hospitality and logistical support during my trips.

My part-time secretary, Valarie Sluss, is due a word of thanks for her excellent help with the typing.

And finally, I would like to express my gratitude to my wife Norma who functions as an equal partner, editor, word processor and encourager and without whose support I would surely collapse. Together we give great praise to God for whom we write. It is our continual prayer that his name will be honored through our writing and through the efforts of worldwide Bible translation.

INTRODUCTION

"Let's do something different," he said. "Perhaps a book of personal remembrances that would give the reader a peek inside your own life and experiences as you've written stories, as well as what has happened in some of the lives of the ethnic peoples you've written about."

I was sitting across the desk from Al Ginty, President of Wycliffe Associates, when we began to brainstorm another book project. Al and I had worked together on several book projects in the past. Each was designed to encourage and help the many lay people, who actively support the ministry of Wycliffe Bible Translators and Wycliffe Associates, gain a more in-depth understanding of the nature and results of Bible translation among the world's ethnic minorities.

I had to confess that the idea of one day writing about some of my traveling encounters was not altogether new. Over the years, as author and photographer-at-large for Wycliffe Bible Translators, I have had several memorable, serendipitous experiences—experiences I thought I would one day chronicle. But that was for "some day." I had too many other projects of greater importance to write.

Then I remembered a letter I received from Ken Jacobs, translator of the Chamula New Testament, telling me how my book, *They Dared to be Different*, prevented his brother from taking his life. I thought also of a story I wrote called "Wound for Wound," and how it had ministered to me when I was going through a bitter disappointment. As I gathered these and several other incidents into this volume of short stories, it seemed to me they mirrored God's grace and mercy while at the same time demonstrated how God uses our frailty for eternal significance.

I therefore offer these remembrances as a gift of love and special tribute to our personal friends and supporters who have stood behind us these past thirty years, as well as to all the friends and supporters of Wycliffe Bible Translators and Wycliffe Associates. It is my prayer that you will be renewed in spirit as you experience the oneness and universality of our common faith in Jesus Christ our Lord.

Hugh Steven
Santa Ana, California

CONTENTS

— 1 —

Wound for Wound

It's been my habit to record in an ongoing journal (not necessarily daily) a variety of the emotions and feelings I've experienced: the death of a loved one, the birth of a grandchild, children leaving home, a special vacation, graduations, birthdays, disappointments, a passage of Scripture that gives courage or new insight, sometimes even prayers of praise and thanksgiving.

I learned early in my writing career that a journal with its appropriate general notations allows me to relive the emotions and circumstances that surrounded an event. I have also learned that my journal allows me to listen to God and reflect on what He has been teaching me.

Some time ago, I experienced a painful moment that has relevance to the following story. Allow me therefore to share a page out of my journal.

For reasons that are still unclear, a book project I have worked on for a year has been canceled. It is an important story, a story that should be told. But now after being three-quarters completed, it is, as they say, "dead in the water."

The long, difficult hours of cataloging hundreds of prayer letters, interview notes and personal letters, the researching, writing, Norma's editing and typing are all suddenly aborted. I wonder if perhaps my career as a writer for Wycliffe is over. After recording the above, I later read some words from 1 Peter 1:7,8 and went back to my journal.

This rejection, this canceling of a year's work is a test of my faith. Peter says, "Rejoice!" But how can I rejoice when the pain is so deep? But I must believe—I do believe—the Word. I am told to rejoice because such tests try my faith to see if it is indeed strong and if it is tested and tried and doesn't break, such faith becomes more valuable than gold. Why? Because one day God will judge each person's actions and choices and attitudes and motives in relation to their faith. What's more, it will be our faith that will garrison our souls and bring honor and glory to our Lord Jesus Christ.

A few days later, I read a passage from Psalm 37 that told me to be patient, to wait, trust and be kind and good to others. It warned me not to let bitterness rob me of a tender, sensitive heart. I was to delight myself in the Lord, rest and relax. Then a friend, who knew of my hurt and who had recently lost his wife to cancer, said simply, "Read Isaiah 64:4 in the Living Bible."

The verse read: "For since the world began, no one has seen or heard of such a God as ours who works for those who wait for him."

These words from the Psalms, Isaiah and 1 Peter truly did effect a healing in my heart. In a few weeks, I was at work on this volume. This was something I had wanted to do for a long time and now I had an opportunity.

When I completed the first story, "Wound for Wound," I was overwhelmed once again by the strength of God's Word to work powerfully in the life of an individual. I was struck with how practical and effective the Word is when believers deliberately choose to take God at his Word and be kind in the face of injustice and disillusionment. I also recognized that here was a word from God to my own heart. An Indonesian brother in Christ had taught me the importance of not returning wound for wound.

> *Do not repay evil with evil or insult with insult . . .*
> *(1 Peter 3:9a NIV).*

There were four of them, and they stepped out of the tropical night shadows each armed with heavy wooden cudgels. They were a hunting party, but not for some Irian Jayan forest animal. They had come rather to settle an old score against a fellow tribe member.

To return evil for evil, an eye for an eye, or wound for wound is, for the Berik people of the northeastern area of Irian Jaya, a cultural norm known as the pay-back system. No matter what the injury to another member of the community, accidental, or not, it is to be returned in similar fashion.

Timbuat crossed the hard-packed red earth of his village to the hut of his friend, Peter Westrum, a Wycliffe Bible translator. Timbuat and Peter had worked together for several years translating the New Testament into the Berik language. Timbuat's personal commitment to Jesus Christ, his quick mind and eagerness for the thousand-plus Berik people to fully understand the meaning of true salvation made him an ideal co-translator.

Timbuat hesitated for just a moment — then made his presence known by calling, "I am here." When Peter came to his doorway, he immediately sensed something

was terribly wrong. Gone was the usual smile and
sparkle in Timbuat's eyes.

Before Peter could ask why, Timbuat said, "I need
medicines. Do you have some for my use?"

"Yes, of course," said Peter. "Come inside and tell me
why you need them." As Timbuat entered, Peter noticed
that most of the men from their small village of about
fifteen families were talking together outside and gathering their spears, heavy hunting cudgels, bows and five-
foot-long arrows.

"What is going on? What are the men doing? Why do
you need medicines?" asked Peter.

"The men of the village want to avenge my brother,"
said Timbuat.

"Avenge your brother? For what reason? What has
happened to him?"

"In his village, four men have fallen upon him and he
has been badly beaten. My friends want to go with me
and give those four men wound for wound, evil for evil,
with the same force they struck my brother. It is the way
of our people to pay back another for an injury, to give
back wound for wound."

"And what about you, Timbuat?" asked Peter. "Do
you agree with them?"

"I am a little confused," said Timbuat. "I know what
the village teaches. I also know that since Jesus Christ
has come to sit in my heart and since we together have
been translating the words of God in Peter's first letter, I
must be a good witness for my Lord. It is for this reason
I must go alone to my brother's village."

"To go alone is dangerous," said Peter. "There are
bad snakes on the trail at night. Maybe the four men,
knowing you have been called to attend to your brother,
will ambush you on the trail. I will go with you."

"I know it is dangerous," said Timbuat, "but I must go alone. Before I go, will you pray with me that whatever happens I will be a good witness for my Lord?"

The moon was full and its pale white light guided Timbuat as he walked along the riverbank and through the tall trees toward his brother's village. Most of his friends and relatives had wanted to go with Timbuat. "We will give them tit for tat, wound for wound, whatever they have given your brother," they said. But Timbuat prevailed. "You must stay here. I am going alone, but the Lord is going with me. Let us see what happens."

Timbuat found his older brother lying unconscious in a one-room thatched hut. He examined him by the light of a small, smoldering fire in the middle of the room and discovered he had a badly broken jaw and several severe wounds. Timbuat cleaned the wounds, applied an antibiotic salve, then bound up his brother's jaw.

Meanwhile, the four attackers stood outside the hut with their friends and relatives, speculating what Timbuat would do when he came outside. "Will he pick a fight? Why has he come unarmed? Where are his friends? Why haven't they come with him? What is going to happen?"

At last Timbuat emerged from the doorway and approached the first of the four men who had attacked his brother. "I want to hold your hand," he said. "I want to thank you for bringing this trial into my life."

Timbuat said the same thing to the other three. They were dumbfounded. "Why," they asked, "why are you talking to us like this?"

"I am one who has Jesus sitting in my heart," said Timbuat. "The Words from God's Book tell us not to repay evil for evil, or wound for wound. In the midst of my great pain, the Lord is strengthening me. This is why I thank you. I did not always have a good life. I had many fears. But then I asked Jesus to sit in my heart and He has given me new encouragement and new strength in my life. I see that these new changes are good and I want the same for you—even you who have done injury to my brother."

Timbuat's forgiving attitude so overwhelmed the four men, they fell at his feet and wept. "Please forgive us," they said through tears of remorse. Before they stood up, they repeated their request and then asked the villagers to forgive them for bringing shame upon them. "It is true," they said. "We see the way you live is better than the way we live. We also would like to follow in this same way."

The next day Timbuat once again crossed the hard-packed red earth of his village to Peter Westrum's hut. When Peter answered Timbuat's greeting this time, he knew something good had happened—the sparkle was back in Timbuat's eyes. Before Peter could ask, Timbuat said, "I have a story to tell you about what the Lord has done."

A New Authority

The book *They Dared to be Different*[2] (hereafter known as *They Dared*) is one of my favorites. It was my hope then, as now, that narrative art would allow the larger Church to experience in a new way their responsibility to missions and their privilege to pray for, support and encourage Bible translation.

Part of the special joy of working on this book had to do with Ken and Elaine Jacobs. From the beginning, their warmth, hospitality, enthusiasm and support encouraged me to plow through the dark tunnels of self-doubt that seem to be part of every writing project. Intuitively, they understood better than most that the nature of historical biography requires the author to select representative elements that give a true but abridged impression of the whole.

And of course, there was the story itself. It had high drama, tragedy, courage and sacrifice—all the great achievements of the human spirit. But there was more. It demonstrated the achievements of the Holy Spirit working in concert with men and women daring to be different in their lifestyles, their worldview and how they wanted to live out their new-found faith in Jesus Christ.

Another reason for the book's memorable place in my heart was the main character, Mariano. In one interview, we came to the place where I had to ask Mariano about the problems in his marriage. Using Ken as an interpreter, I said, "Mariano, if this is too painful for you, don't tell me."

"No," he said, "I see you are a man with a straight heart. I know you would never harm me." It was surely one of the finest compliments I have ever received!

But perhaps the reason *They Dared* is memorable for me is because God chose to use this simple story in a way that is totally outside the realm of anything I could have possibly imagined.

One day in April 1979, I found this letter in my mail box:

> Dear Hugh and Norma:
>
> If you wrote the book, *They Dared to be Different,* only to meet the need of the one person I'm going to tell you a little about, it would have been worth all your effort. Oh! how Dave blesses you. I just had to sit down at my old machine and send you these words of encouragement and Christian gratitude.
>
> Elaine and I gave a copy of your book to my brother Dave and his wife Jan. Dave is much younger than I. Ever since he left home and married he has been "master of his own life." In no way did he want to come under the authority of Christ.
>
> Everything seemed to go Dave's way. He had four children who respected him. He had built the largest home in his area. He came to own his own successful business. As he put it to me, "I had done everything right to make me happy."

But Dave was far from happy. His world was falling apart. His business began to deteriorate and had to be sold. His new home had to be sacrificed to pay bills. His married life became strained as he reacted in bitterness to those around him. Inner guilt and resentment drove Dave to even deeper failure. Separation from his family and divorce was being discussed as the only alternative.

I'm sure God used many things to bring Dave to his senses, but, as he related it to me, it was the unimaginable peace that struggling, failing Mariano embraced that was more than he could endure. Dave said to me, "Ken, I wept uncontrollably through whole chapters of that book. I longed, even craved for what Mariano had."

Dave then called me by phone and asked if he could come over. I had no idea how broken and ready Dave was for healing. He said to me during the late-hour conversation, "Ken, I want the peace that Mariano has more than I want anything in all the world."

It was obvious that his hunger and thirst for the God of Mariano was very real. Before he drove home that night, we had knelt in our living room and prayed together. "Ken, I don't know how to pray," he said. "Tell God what you have been telling me," I replied. The dam of self-sufficiency and inner protection broke as Dave began to verbalize his inner self to God, the God of Mariano.

Since that wonderful night a few days ago now, Dave and I have been together off and on.

It is obvious that Dave has a new authority in his life—the Helper of Mariano. Dave told me that Jan was reading the book and had said that she wanted to call me and talk about it. During one of their conversations together she had said that perhaps their relationship could begin to heal.

There is more to tell but this will give you joy.

Sincerely,

Ken

Several months after receiving this letter, Ken and Elaine came through the Wycliffe office in Huntington Beach, California, and shared with me the "more" of his brother's encounter with the book *They Dared.* Said Ken, "When Elaine and I came home for a short furlough, we were invited over to Dave's home for dinner. During the course of our visit, Elaine turned to me and asked if I had given Dave a copy of the book. There were two copies in the trunk of my car, but it was a cold, blowing, wintry night and I didn't feel like getting up and going outside. I made no reply.

"Perhaps a half hour later, Elaine again turned and said, 'Ken, give Dave and Jan a book before we go.' Reluctantly I donned my heavy coat and went out to the car to get a copy. About three days later Dave called and asked if he could come over and see me."

"I've been reading the book," he said. "I've read it from cover to cover. Couldn't put it down. I have to tell you I wept through whole chapters of the book. Ken, you know the kind of life I've had. One of the biggest homes in the community. Three expensive cars sitting in the driveway. Tonight I drove up here in a beat-up Volkswagen Bug that's not worth more than a hundred bucks. I have always run my life my own way and now I

have run it into shambles. That Mariano has everything!
I have nothing! I crave what that man has. I long for it.
It's not money I need. What I need is a new authority in
my life. I've got to have it because if I don't, I'm going to
kill myself. I hate everybody, everybody hates me and I
hate myself!"

What Ken didn't know and wouldn't know for some
time was that this was no idle boast. His brother's hate
for himself, his own jealousy and internal strife had
driven him to the point of desperation. Dave was
indeed planning to take his own life.

"Dave," said Ken, "let me share how Mariano helped
me translate a beatitude. It's the words of Jesus where
He says, 'Blessed are the poor in spirit, for theirs is the
kingdom of heaven.' In Chamula we can't say this.
First, because the Chamulas don't have a word for
'blessed.' And second, the words 'poor' and 'spirit' don't
collocate. That is, one can talk about a 'poor' day, or
'poor' people, but a spirit can't be poor.

"To get around this problem, the verse was translated,
'How wonderful for the man who realizes in his heart
that there is nothing he can do to save himself. The man
who realizes in his heart there is nothing he can do to
save himself is already experiencing the government of
heaven.' "

And then under the guidance of the Holy Spirit, Ken
made a statement he had heard Mariano and the
Chamula believers use in their efforts to explain the
reality of how a human being can have a personal
relationship with the Living God.

"Dave, if Mariano were here tonight he would say to
you, 'Dave, God sees you well because of what Christ
has done.' " Ken then explained how the Chamulas
could not in typical Western Christian jargon under-

stand what it meant to "receive" Christ. Again it was the problem of collocation.

"In Chamula one can receive a concrete object, like an ox or a machete, but not a person. Therefore, when a Chamula says, 'God sees you well because of what Christ has done,' this means, 'If you take Me seriously, I [Jesus] make Myself responsible to handle all your sin. I died for you. I am offering to govern your life. I will write my laws on your heart and your mind. I will take you from where you are now to where I want you to go. That is good news or bad news depending on how you choose.' "

The phrase, "God sees you well because of what Christ has done," lodged deep into Dave's consciousness. Just as he identified with Mariano as one who like himself needed a new authority in his life, so Dave was open to Ken when he said at length, "Dave, why don't you pray?"

"Pray? I don't know how. I never pray."

For a moment, Ken didn't know how to respond. Then he said, "Well, if you can stand just one more example from Chamula, I'll tell you what the Chamula Christians say to a person much like yourself who wants to know how to find God, or as the Chamulas say, 'Tell us what to do to find something for our hearts.' They say, 'Just tell God what you are telling us,' in this case, what you are telling me."

With his hand on Dave's shoulder, both men knelt beside the sofa. It was there Dave told God how he had lived his life his own way, how he had lived it independently of God and how he had made a mess of it. Said Ken, "Dave began telling God what he had been telling me. Out of his deep inner soul, he began to pour out all the things he had kept hidden for so long—things he wouldn't have admitted to anyone, even himself— all came tumbling out between hot, wet tears . . . and Dave walked smack into the kingdom of God."

Several days later Ken phoned his brother. As he dialed the number, he experienced a twinge of uneasiness. He was aware of some of Dave's past "stunts" and various pretexts, but when Dave answered the phone, Ken knew immediately something dramatic had happened in his life. Boldly, Ken asked a leading question. "Dave, how come you have Christ as a new authority in your life?" Dave hesitated for a moment, then said, "Two reasons. One, I need Him. And two, I chose Him. I suppose in reality it was He Who chose me!"

"What about going back to running your life the way you did before?"

"Oh, Ken, that's the way back to hell," said Dave. "I am now under a new authority, a new direction and I want to keep it that way."

Dave was and is today as good as his word. Two years after their late-night meeting, Ken again had occasion to visit his brother. As they reminisced, Dave reminded Ken of how appreciative he was for the ministry of the book *They Dared to be Different* in his own life. "It was this book, after all," said Dave, "that first made me realize I couldn't handle my own sins—that I needed the God of Mariano!"

* * * * *

Curiously, the very week I received the letter from Ken telling me about his brother, we entertained a couple we hadn't seen in over ten years. During a lull in the conversation they said, "We want to tell you how your book, *They Dared to be Different,* ministered in our lives."

Apparently the wife had pretty much decided to get a divorce, that it was over for them. "And then one weekend we went to a retreat," said the wife. "Others thought this would help us, but I was in no mood to sit in lectures on how to be a better wife or how to have a happy marriage. I decided to go to the bookstore and it was there I saw your book, *They Dared to be Different*. It seemed innocuous enough. A missionary story, I thought. Nothing here about how to have a better marriage or thirteen ways to please your husband! The last thing I wanted was a book on how to save my marriage!

"I began reading and when I came to the place in the book where Mariano's wife Estumina, with great courage and simple trust in the God of her new faith, reached out in forgiveness and reconciliation after all that Mariano had done, the Spirit of God just seemed to zap me.

"I was a woman who conducted Bible studies, who had gone overseas to tell others about the Good News of Jesus Christ, and now I was suddenly faced with the reality that I was living my life pretty much as I wanted to live it. My faith, which should have made a difference in my outlook, lifestyle and choices, was being pushed aside. Through this story of two non-sophisticated people, I was being challenged in a new way to submit my will to a higher authority. That book was the turning point in our marriage."

"I appreciate you sharing that remarkable story," I said. "While I am writing a book, and certainly after the book is written, I feel very much like a bystander to my work. I feel as if I am standing on the sidelines watching the Spirit of God do his office work. I feel quite peripheral—almost extraneous, like a mirage. I am ever conscious that He must increase and I indeed must decrease."

* * * * *

Several years after *They Dared* was published, I returned to Las Casas to research and write an update on what had happened to the Chamula Church in the intervening years. From the beginning of my association with the Chamula believers, I had the highest regard for their steadfast resolve to place their confidence and trust in Jesus Christ in the face of severe persecution.

In 1964, the Chamula Church began with two men, Domingo Hernandez and Miguel Gomez Hernandez who worked in Ken's garden in Las Casas. Within a year, four other men came to personal faith in Christ, and these grew to 35. Between 1965 and 1969 about 130 men, women and children dared to be different, to examine God's Word as it was being translated for them. All had been challenged to trust and believe in the one true God as their Rightful Owner. This they did in the face of social and political censorship, confiscation of lands, torture and murder.

For the first ten years of their assignment among the Chamulas, however, Ken and Elaine saw no visible interest in the Good News about Jesus Christ. On one occasion, a group of visiting pastors from the United States stood with Ken on a hill on the outskirts of Las Casas. In the distance, they could see the rugged hill country and the valley filled with a soft blue haze. Clinging to the hillsides were small Chamula huts with thin streams of smoke coming out of their thatched roofs. As Ken explained his hope for the Chamulas, one of the pastors, with a critical edge to his voice, turned to Ken and said, "What in the world are *you* doing to evangelize the Chamulas?"

"Well," said Ken, "it all depends on what you mean by 'evangelize.' During my Bible school days in Minneapolis, I used to knock on doors. That strategy doesn't work here. You have to present the Gospel through a different grid. In the first place, we can't even live among the Chamulas. They would kill us if we tried. And if we went in for a visit to 'knock on doors,' we wouldn't get past the second hut before a machete or muzzle-loaded gun would be at our backs.

"If you mean by 'evangelize,' do we rent a public address system and gather a large crowd for a religious meeting, what would I say? Chamulas never share new or different information publicly. If you have something new to share, you confide it to a relative who you hope will not kill you for believing something different from the norm. If that's what you mean by evangelizing the Chamulas, then Elaine and I aren't doing one blessed thing.

"But let me tell you what is going on. There are a half-dozen Chamula men who come regularly to work in my garden. There is a family living on our property and from them we have learned and are learning the language. If I'm able to talk to one of them, I can talk to all 50,000. As I talk to the men and explain they are 'seen well by God' and tell them about all that Jesus Christ has done for them, it is my hope and prayer that when one person begins to understand this new message, he will have the courage to risk his life by sharing this message with his relatives and friends. From that spark will come a flame and then a fire."

On the Sunday I returned to observe what had happened during the seven years since I first chronicled the Chamula story, I attended their first-ever baptismal service. The scene looked like something straight out of the New Testament—like how I perceive the feeding of the 5,000 may have looked. On a long, sloping hill with green grass that grazing sheep had manicured to putting-green perfection, sat over 3,000 people. I was struck first by a sea of rich blue head coverings that fell over the women's white blouses brightly embroidered in red. Most of the men wore their handsome off-white wool panchos and white sombreros.

This green hillside had the feel of a great cathedral. People sang and read the Scriptures. Several speakers explained how, in obedience to God's Word, seventy of their number had voluntarily asked to be baptized in the cold mountain stream that flowed through the gentle hillside.

In reality, Ken and Elaine have spent no time doing mass evangelism. Elaine brought her microscope and did medical work. This brought a large number of Chamulas to her backyard in Las Casas. Most were unable to find healing through the traditional shaman or witch doctor. At Elaine's invitation, the Chamulas would peer through her microscope to look at the parasites that were making them ill. Since Chamulas wouldn't accept what they couldn't see, Elaine explained that the parasites they saw in the microscope were making them ill. When she then prescribed certain medicines to counteract the parasites, the people followed her instruction, became well, and began little by little to trust her. And thus when she explained that spiritual sickness, like physical sickness, needed to be treated, the Chamulas were ready to listen to the story of the Great Physician Who could heal their sins.

It was a small beginning, but Elaine, like Ken,

patiently answered each question as if it was the first time it had been asked. "It was a slow process," said Ken. "I would go over a certain passage and the men would say, 'I doubt if that can be true.' But as I repeated the story over and over, it began to sink deep into their hearts. It just took time for them to realize that God had made Himself responsible to handle their sins. They had never heard of such a thing before."

After observing firsthand the redemptive work of God's grace among the Chamulas, Ken Jacobs has arrived at a conclusion. "My conclusion," said Ken, "is that we translators are not called to *interpret* the New Testament. We are called to simply *translate* the message of God's grace and love as recorded in the New Testament with as much clarity and force as was experienced by the original hearers of the message. The Holy Spirit will then communicate his Word to the people through their own unique cultural grid and when the pure Word of God touches them, the people will respond and believe."

This is exactly what happened among the Chamulas. As of this writing, the Chamula Church has grown to over 10,000 believers and continues to grow. There are four major congregations with standing room only on any given Sunday in one church that holds 2,000-plus people. The second edition of 15,000 copies of the Chamula New Testament is currently being printed. God's Word is indeed strong and sharp and powerful!

— 3 —

Six Flies, Warm Apple Pop
and Reflections

The events of the Chamula baptismal were fresh in my mind as I walked into an obscure storefront "restaurant" in the town of Tuxtla in southern Mexico. The day before, I had taken a late-afternoon bus down the two-hour tortuous switchback road from Las Casas. I had spent the night in a second-class hotel near the bus station.

It was 7:00 a.m. and I had two hours to wait until a microbus (converted VW Wagon) could take me to the Tuxtla airport where I would fly to Mexico City and then home to Los Angeles. I sat down at a table nearest the window that opened directly onto the street across from the bus depot. In an effort to absorb and synthesize what had happened during my revisit among the Chamulas, I took out my steno pad and began to scribble. After many years of writing, I've noticed an interesting relationship between taking pen in hand and making marks on paper. This physical act has a way of stimulating my memory and creativity. And so, much like a musician who warms up his instrument before a performance or a singer who vocalizes, I will share, along with my reflections, some of my non-verbal vocalizing on that hot humid morning.

As I sit down, I am immediately aware of my table. It is a simple rough-cut pine table with squared wooden legs. One or two of the legs are shorter than the others. It wobbles. I am also aware of my chair. The seat is covered with a heavy plastic and has several tears, all of which are repaired with the miracle product, Scotch Tape.

My table is covered with a sticky plastic tablecloth. Six flies flit back and forth between my table and the plastic-covered chairs at the next one. The paint on the walls and high ceiling of this "restaurant" is faded blue-purple. This is accented by dull canary yellow wooden shutters on paneless windows.

A single overhead fan tries in vain to dissipate the rising humidity and heat that is beginning to seep through the doors and windows. At one table over sit four rumpled men who look as if they have slept in their clothes. All sport Arafat beards. One rubs the sleep out of his eyes; the others sit silently staring into empty space.

My host for the moment is a timid young man. I ask for the menu. "All we have to offer is drinks," he says. I remind him that there were some eggs sitting on the counter. "Oh, yes," he says, "we can give you scrambled eggs mixed with Spanish sausage or ham." I choose the ham.

While he shuffles over to tell the cook what I want, I examine more closely just how this restaurant operates. The mother orchestrates the day's events. She makes change out of her purse that sits on top of the cash register. Unsmiling, and with the intensity of a captain of industry, she constantly gives out orders and directions to the table boy and a cook of undiscernable age. Behind the counter her six- or seven-, maybe even eight-year-old daughter, who wears a flower print dress, rests her chin on the counter. Her hair is raven-wing black and she has large brown eyes that peer out from behind a cute oval face. She looks at me. I look at her. She smiles with embarrassment.

Grandmother is here, too. She wears a white peasant blouse with a gray shawl slung over one shoulder. Two gold coins made into earrings dangle from slightly stretched earlobes. She has steel-gray hair and deep, weathered lines etch her bronzed face. She appears to have been the kind of woman who may have ridden with Pancho Villa, and by the way her shawl is slung across her chest, it might just as well be a brace of bandoliers. As I observe this microcosm, I wonder how they would have responded to the question the Chamulas voluntarily put to themselves. Namely, "Are you in the process of attaining God's goal for your life? Because when you find the goal God wants for your life, your heart will explode with gladness."

"Explode with gladness." What a metaphor to express this new concrete reality of God Who took the initiative to meet a people and to transform them, to give them new unity of purpose, new faith, new hope. This encounter with the living God brought about a disentanglement of a whole series of idolatries; a freedom from a tyrannical government that had cordoned off its society in order to maintain control.

Christian Chamulas had become a people without status, or political clout—exiles in their own country. Many fled only with what they could carry in their hands and on their backs. Most were babes in their faith—wholly dependent upon God—but it was because they were weak that they had become strong. Having nothing they had everything.

Long ago the Apostle Paul wrote some words that the Chamulas understand perfectly. ". . . for Christ's sake, I delight in weakness, in insults, in hardships, in persecutions, in difficulties. For when I am weak, then I am strong" (2 Corinthians 12:10 NIV).

Ah, in the middle of my scribbling, the young waiter has brought my breakfast. Since I don't like coffee, or more correctly, coffee doesn't like me, I order the local apple pop. "Is it cold?" I ask. It's not. I'm content to wash down the eggs and ham and the tortillas (four served on a small plastic saucer) with the warm apple pop. This, after all, is part of what traveling in rural Mexico is all about.

All six flies are still here and I eat with one hand at the ready. In vain I try to destroy them. I'm happy just to be able to swish them away when they creep too close to my pop and eggs.

As I continue to reflect on the Chamulas, I remember the impression I had about their becoming truly Christian. They had lost nothing of their "Chamulaness." In fact, because of this personal relationship between God and man, leaders emerged who were working together to restore what selfish men had torn apart—restoration between husband and wife, son and father, and restoration within a society that had once lost its meaning and significance and was now looking forward to the future with a new awareness of who they were. Salt and light had come, and with it came a hitherto-unknown expression of peace and joy. This was clearly evident in the Chamula communal celebrations, like the baptismal service which had replaced the fiesta.

In the days before my career with Wycliffe, my understanding of a "fiesta" was what Hollywood had

erroneously depicted on the screen. This usually con-
sisted of fireworks, street dancing, a romantic interlude
between a beautiful young woman and a handsome
well-groomed suitor. In reality, fiestas are religious
functions that include fireworks as part of their "worship,"
but they are also social and political functions—often
violent.

Little of the Hollywood-depicted merriment is present
at most fiestas in rural Mexico, Guatemala and generally throughout Latin America. The end result of most
fiestas are drunken stupors for large segments of the
participants. Many bankrupt themselves from over-
spending. Long-standing feuds that simmer but remain
controlled under normal social constraints, erupt in
violence and often death when drink loosens inhibitions.

I've been scribbling for some time now and I set
down my pen and lift my eyes once more to observe.

Grandmother hasn't smiled since she slid into her
chair. There is a faint hint of a smile when her
granddaughter, the one with the big brown eyes and
flower print dress, serves her a large cup of *cafe con
leche* (coffee with hot milk) and then sits down beside
her. She also serves Grandmother sweetbreads in a
plastic basket. I wonder why the young waiter didn't tell
me about this option! Grandmother dunks a roll into
her coffee and begins to munch.

Mother joins the little table. She too has a large cup of
cafe con leche. The cup is flowered with a brown zig-zag
crack and a large chip out of one side. She stirs her *cafe
con leche* a long time before drinking. I can't understand
all that is being said. I'm not really listening.

Suddenly the trio is joined by a handsome young
man—perhaps seventeen or eighteen. He wears a
freshly-pressed Levi shirt, blue cords—also freshly

pressed—and tan cowboy boots. This is, after all, ranch country. He joins in the conversation, smiles a lot, and appears content and relaxed. Grandmother looks up. She's pleased and proud and she smiles.

That's what had impressed me about the baptismal service. There were smiles, great rich, warm smiles. And when there were no physical smiles on their countenances, one could sense an inner warmth and energy that would, with the slightest excuse, explode into an expression of joy.

I've finished my breakfast now and think about leaving. My steno pad is full of markings that I have no idea how I will, if ever, use.

I ask the young waiter for my bill. He asks the mother. She whispers, "Eighty pesos." At the then-rate of exchange it amounted to eighty U.S. cents. As the mother makes change, I wonder about their lives. Are they as complex and desperate as many of my compatriots? I wonder about their spiritual lives and about their relationship to Christ. Mother wears a heavy pearl cross. Is this a clue?

I smile at those who have served me, thank them, and walk to the door. The world outside the restaurant is now alive with activity. A big diesel bus revs its motor and spews brown-black exhaust into the street. Cars honk horns, a street vendor pushes an ice-cream cart with a row of little bells. He picks his favorite spot near the passenger entrance to the bus depot. A street sweeper with a long-handled broom made from dried twigs scrapes the street litter into piles along the curb. Inside the restaurant, no one notices.

As I walk back to my hotel, I wonder if my musing about the Chamula baptismal service hadn't been too Pollyannish. Were my observations objective or too optimistic? I don't normally subscribe to the old cliché of some Christian workers who would identify believers from non-believers by the "smiles" on their faces. Few of us can sustain a happy countenance all the time. Life isn't that happy. And if any group of people know the truth of such a statement, it is certainly the Chamula Church. Of course, not all the Chamulas at the baptismal service were smiling. But there was, as I described earlier, an energy, a joy that was neither too optimistic nor too pessimistic. Later, as I thought further on that day, I was reminded of a passage J.B. Phillips once wrote in describing the young New Testament Church in Acts. He, better than I could ever write, captures the way I felt about what had happened among the Chamula Church and what that baptismal service was all about.

> Unless we happen to have studied ancient history, we may not have realized how remarkable are the bright hopes of the early band of Christians. The surrounding pagan world was dark; it was full of fear, cruelty, and superstition. For the most part the old religions had failed. Human life had become cheap; common morality was in many cases very lightly regarded; and belief in a world to come was almost nonexistant ... But in the Young Church there was gay and indomitable hope. Nothing could quench this hope, for these men and women now knew through Christ what God was like, and they now knew for certain that death was a defeated enemy. While the pagan world had largely become sodden with self-indulgence and ridden by the fear of death, the brave new fellowship of

believers in Christ was a light and a flame in the darkness; it was a fellowship of hope.[3]

As I thought about all that had occurred and all that had come to the Chamulas through the instrumentation of Ken and Elaine, my mind went back to a serious incident that almost destroyed them from ever becoming the vehicle through whom the "fellowship of hope" came about. It happened on a lonely bridge in Oklahoma. . . .

— 4 —

A Very Present Help
on a Bridge of Pain

It was January 1954. Ken and Elaine Jacobs' official permission to remain outside Mexico had almost expired. They had taken their nine-year-old daughter Joyce to their hometown of Minneapolis for emergency medical treatment and were now returning to Mexico and their new assignment among the Chamulas. Their only chance of making their deadline was to drive all night to the border.

The Jacob's car was cozy and warm and, in spite of pulling a two-wheeled luggage trailer, the car sped easily along Oklahoma Highway 81. Tired from his fifteen-plus hours of driving, Ken had turned the wheel over to Elaine and stretched out in the back seat to sleep.

Nine-year-old daughter Joyce dozed beside Elaine in the front seat. At 3:30 a.m., about fifty miles from the Texas-Oklahoma line, the roads became slick in a thick blanket of fog. Cautiously, Elaine drove down the highway for several miles when suddenly out of the fog loomed a bridge. She slowed the car. About halfway across, the car and trailer began to skid on the icy steel bridge surface. More out of reflex than reason, Elaine applied the brakes and yelled for Ken.

Immediately Elaine felt a hard jerk and a thump as the car and trailer jackknifed and slid across the road to the lefthand side. The back end of the trailer and the nose of the car were both snug up against a concrete barricade.

Before Elaine could explain to Ken that they were on a bridge, he leapt out of the lefthand car door, still groggy from sleep. For a split second, he paused to survey the situation as he stood inside the "U" formed by the car and trailer. Then, apparently thinking the barricade separated a divided highway, he placed both hands on the waist-high barricade and vaulted over.

The only sound Elaine heard was Ken's breath being expelled as if he had received a terrible punch in the stomach. Kicking open her door that was slightly stuck from the accident, she sprang to the barricade and peered over the edge into empty blackness. Frantically she called to Ken. There was no answer.

Elaine returned to the car for a flashlight. It wasn't where it was supposed to be. Half running, half slipping, she raced to the trunk and felt around the luggage. No flashlight. "O Lord," she prayed, "I know the flashlight is in the car someplace. Please help me find it." From the trunk Elaine searched under the front seat. Can of oil, rag, whisk broom, crumbs, ice scraper. *How ironic*, she thought. *The first time in our lives we carry a five-cell flashlight and now I can't find it.*

Suddenly her fingers touched cold metal. "Thank You, Lord" whispered Elaine.

Peering over the barricade, the beam of yellow light picked up Ken's crumpled form thirty feet below. "O Lord!" murmured Elaine, "he's dead!" Quickly grabbing a blanket and pillow and with Joyce in tow still rubbing the sleep from her eyes, they started down toward Ken. Tangled underbrush pulled at their clothes and scratched their legs as they made their way down the bank at the end of the bridge. For an instant Elaine paused when she came to a creek. She had no idea how deep it was. Carefully, with Joyce in her arms, she stepped into the cold, dark water and started across. About midway, the water came halfway up her 5'3" frame. It was the deepest part.

Elaine continued wading until she came to where Ken's twisted form lay on a sandbar mid-stream. Still not sure if he was dead or alive, she spread the blanket over him and gently placed the pillow under his head. As she brought Ken's outstretched arms under the blanket, he moaned.

At that moment Elaine knew what she had to do. "Joyce, honey," explained Elaine, "Mommy's going to get someone to help us. You stay with Daddy. I can't leave the flashlight. I'll need it to flag down a car."

Elaine made her way through the creek and back up the bank of tangled underbrush to the jackknifed car and trailer. Slipping in behind the wheel, she turned on the ignition. For the second time that night, she asked God to help her. Praying as she put the car in reverse, Elaine gave the wheel a hard left turn. The trailer scraped the barricade. Then she shifted into low and with a firm grip on the wheel (no power steering), turned it as far to the right as she could. She gently eased down on the gas pedal. Miraculously, the wheels didn't slip or slide. In moments, she was across the bridge and driving down the highway in search of help.

About two miles from the bridge, Elaine spotted bright headlights in her rearview mirror. Immediately, she pulled over to the side, got out and began to frantically wave her flashlight up and down. Two trucks pulled to a stop.

Calmly she explained her problem to the drivers. Soon one truck driver was speeding on his way for an ambulance; the other turned his rig around and took Elaine back to the bridge.

When Elaine returned to the bridge and started down the bank, instead of tangled underbrush, she ran into barbed wire. No stranger to barbed wire fences, Elaine crawled through and waded across the creek, but to her horror she couldn't find Ken.

Realizing she must have taken a wrong turn, she retraced her steps and finally found Ken as she had left him—except that Joyce was not there. Fearing the worst, she began to shout her name.

"Mommy! Mommy! I am up here." Elaine looked up to see the flashing lights of a police car on the bridge. Later, Elaine learned that Ken had come to, found himself alone with Joyce, and in his delirium, told her to go for help. Taught always to obey, Joyce went. To this day Elaine doesn't know how she managed to cross the creek and scramble up the bank in the dark.

Secure in the knowledge that Joyce was being cared for, Elaine turned her attention to Ken. As part of her training for pioneer Bible translation, she had taken first-aid and related medical courses. A superficial examination revealed that both Ken's arms and several of his left ribs were broken. Later it was discovered that many of his ribs on his right side and four vertebrae were also fractured.

But what concerned Elaine most were Ken's broken ribs. When he began to cough up blood, her worst fears were realized. The broken ribs had collapsed his lung causing internal bleeding. He was drowning in his own blood!

As Ken lay dying, the shock was almost too much for Elaine. Much later she said, "I had to fight to control my own body. I was desperate. I didn't want to lose Ken. I had already lost one husband within a year of my wedding. (Her first husband was killed in Korea.) Through the difficult years of adjustment before I met Ken, I had come to understand that God wasn't a magic genie who would grant every wish. But I knew also that He would never forsake me. I knew He had helped me find the flashlight and get the car and trailer back to the right side of the road. And it wasn't just coincidence that two trucks came along when I needed them."

And so with her hands gently cupped around Ken's face, Elaine waited for the ambulance and prayed. "Lord, Ken and I believe You called us to the Chamula people. They don't know your Word. They don't know the true meaning of spiritual freedom that comes from knowing You. But now Ken is dying. I need him. Joyce needs him, and we believe the Chamula people need him. So if You still have work for us to do, Lord, we want to do it. Please don't let Ken die."

At 5:30 a.m., two hours after Ken's fall off the bridge, he was picked up by an ambulance crew and driven to a small Oklahoma hospital. Cold and wet from their several creek crossings, Elaine and Joyce were put to bed by the attending hospital staff.

Meanwhile, technicians took x-rays of Ken and the nurses tried to make him comfortable. At 9:00 a.m., the resident doctor woke Elaine and told her they were moving Ken to McBride Clinic in Oklahoma City. "We have to go into the chest cavity and draw off blood," explained the doctor. "We can't handle this delicate procedure here. We have to take him immediately. The ambulance is waiting."

There wasn't even time to retrieve their parked car out on the highway. More dead than alive, Ken was wheeled into the waiting ambulance, and with sirens wailing, whisked 140 miles to McBride.

What followed for Ken was pneumonia, pleurisy and five painful months of slow healing. For Elaine, it was the day-to-day vigil of watching Ken slowly regain his strength.

Some weeks after Ken's accident, Elaine happened to meet the ambulance driver who had picked up Ken after the fall and who had driven them to McBride. He asked about Ken and was pleased to learn he was improving and would indeed live.

"I never really expected your husband to live," said the ambulance driver. "And, ma'am, I've seen a lot of people who had to face what you did, but I've never seen one like you. You didn't fuss or cry; you just stayed cool."

"Thank you," said Elaine, smiling. "What else can you do at a time like that but trust the Lord?"

The rest, of course, is history. As the years passed, Ken and Elaine and the Chamulas learned over and over again what it meant to trust God. For the Chamulas, it meant drastic revolution in their thinking. For Ken and Elaine, it meant relearning that indeed God was not a magic genie to lift them out of their troubles. Rather, they all learned together that in the daily strain and pain and complex problems of life, God is a very present help in time of trouble.

— 5 —

Dividing to Conquer

N ow that you are back in the homeland, you can't expect our church to continue your support."

He was a longtime friend, now a successful pastor of a vigorous city church. He, with his wife and family, were vacationing and had come to share a summer barbecue in our backyard in Southern California. I had just finished explaining that I had recently been assigned to work out of the U.S. Home Division office as Wycliffe's full-time author and photographer-at-large —"at-large" meaning that I wasn't confined to one geographical spot, but would travel to collect material and photographs from all Wycliffe fields.

"I don't understand," I said.

"It has to do with front lines," he said. "Our people would rather support someone who is involved directly with the people."

"I suppose I shouldn't argue with established church policy to support only those who are on the so-called front lines," I said. "However, I need to tell you I couldn't do what I've been assigned to do here at home if I hadn't first had eleven years' field experience in Mexico. And if I was still on the field, I couldn't do what I've been asked to do here!"

"I see your point," he said, "but don't you think Wycliffe should pay your salary now that you are in a home office?"

"Curiously, you've raised two important issues that confuse many people unfamiliar with Wycliffe policy," I said. "First, it doesn't matter if I'm stationed in California or Cameroon, Pennsylvania or the Philippines. No matter what my assignment or geographical location, I'm still part of the Wycliffe team.

"Wycliffe's purpose is to translate God's Word into every language of the world where a translation is needed. What I do as a writer, what our accountants do, what our printers, nurses, pilots, mechanics, secretaries, house parents, our base teachers and the teachers at our SIL schools do, is all part of Wycliffe's stated goal of providing the Scriptures for Bibleless peoples of the world.

"Second, as far as being paid for what I do, that would be nice, but Wycliffe is a faith mission and provides no guaranteed allowance or income for its members. Each member is required to look to God for his or her temporal needs. As I understand Scripture, God generally works through his people—the church—to supply such needs." (Parenthetically, Wycliffe does carefully forward all monies designated by a donor to the specific Wycliffe member. The donor then receives a tax receipt.)

I was about to explain how Wycliffe members themselves had voted to contribute ten percent of all monies they receive back to the organization for operational costs, part going to the member's home division and part to his field, when my wife reminded me the hamburgers were burning on the grill!

That little backyard drama took place more than sixteen years ago. Since then I've struggled, like others in the Wycliffe family, to communicate to our prayer and financial backers that Wycliffe's home-assigned personnel still need the support and understanding of their home church, friends and constituents. A Wycliffe worker who accepts a home assignment is a valuable team member. Not only are they necessary in their backup positions, but often they are used in important developmental positions. One Wycliffe couple serving in Mexico volunteered themselves to Wycliffe's Canadian Home Division in order to develop a Canada-wide communications program.

Dr. James Dean, current Canadian Home Division Director, and his wife Gladys spent many years in Papua New Guinea and Indonesia directing and opening up these and other Wycliffe fields. The success and forward momentum of the Canadian Division is due in a large measure to Dr. Dean's wide field experience. It is this sensitive understanding of Wycliffe's unique structure, policies and field operations that make him such an indispensable asset to a home division program.

When Pat MacLeod took a home assignment following the sudden death of her husband Tom, she discovered a whole new world of service. The MacLeods had completed the New Testament for the Philippines' Dumagat people and were awaiting its publication when Tom died from a liver complaint brought about by infectious hepatitis. During her period of adjustment, Pat took a six-month furlough in her home division office.

"I really didn't know what I would be doing," said Pat, "I just wanted to help. For years I thought that the people who worked in the home office were the ones who somehow didn't make it on the field, or had returned from the field because they didn't fit in. I was terribly mistaken! I discovered a group of people who were working with the same sense of call, commitment and dedication that our fellow translators and support workers displayed in the Philippines. Everyone, from the person who kept the office clean, right through each department, knew they were in some way contributing to the overall task of Bible translation."

Not long ago I was reminded of that backyard barbecue when a Wycliffe colleague wrote, "A home-assigned person may be asked to speak less and less. Reason? People would rather hear a report from the front lines. Many have reduced income because the Church believes the office pays them for their service." All of us understand how strategic and important it is to have workers on the "front lines," but, humanly speaking, little could happen on those front lines without proper logistical support from dedicated, trained and committed workers in the homeland.

In 1 Samuel 25:13, King David divided his fighting force in two. Half of the men were ordered to strap on their swords; the other half were ordered to stay by the supplies. Both groups of fighting men were needed to realize victory.

To achieve Wycliffe's goal of forwarding the translation of God's Word into every language, we, too, need to divide our forces. To "conquer," we need those who are willing to strap on their swords—to be on the "front lines"—and we also need those who are willing to stay by the "supplies."

The Book Speaks Tepehuan

The dedication was an historical landmark—for the first time in history the Tepehuan people of Northern Mexico were to receive the New Testament in their own language. It was a simple dedicatory celebration, and while only a handful of outsiders, including myself and approximately 230 Tepehuan people witnessed the event, God saw it and was pleased. It is man after all, not God, who despises small things.

God was pleased because at last a door of understanding was being opened to a people who heretofore knew little of the mystery of the Gospel of Christ. And God was pleased with two families—Wycliffe translators Burt and Marvel Bascom, and Loreto and Narcisa Herrera. For, in spite of a serious heart ailment and the responsibilities of her husband and family, Narcisa became Burt's co-translator and gave herself unreservedly to the translation of the New Testament.

God was also pleased with the faithfulness of those who prayed and financially supported the Bascoms in their long career as translators and as teachers who have helped train hundreds of Wycliffe workers at yearly SIL schools. (It was a special joy for Norma and me in the summer of 1985 when Burt and Marvel taught linguistics to our son Lee and his wife Paula as twenty-nine years earlier they had been our teachers!)

The following story is a tribute to all such supporters and to all, like the Bascoms and Herreras, who have been faithful and steadfast in their commitment, even in the face of difficulty, discouragement and hardship.

Unsmiling and flanked by other unsmiling members of his council, the Tepehuan Indian chief sat down. Not on a chair, or a stool, or a bench, but on the edge of a low, dirt-encrusted stone wall that buttressed a nearby adobe church. To the 8,000-plus Tepehuan Indians who live on the outskirts of Baborigame (Fig Tree Village), a sawmill town in the state of Chihahua, Mexico, this small, unassuming grandfather-of-a-man had veto power in matters religious and political among the Tepehuan people.

The chief, known as "the general," leaned forward and placed his hands on his knees. It was a simple gesture, but the onlookers knew the general had reached a verdict. Before him stood a tall, angular man in his mid-thirties—Loreto Herrera. Unlike the general who was supported by councilmen and a sympathetic audience, Loreto stood absolutely alone. Alone physically, and alone ideologically.

"Loreto," said the general, "you have asked my permission for the last time. My answer is no! It is the same answer that the council gave you the last time you asked to hold this meeting you call a dedication service."

"My General," said Loreto, "I speak not only for myself. Many Tepehuan people out on their ranches are anxious to see this Book—this New Testament Señor Burt Bascom has put into the Tepehuan language. All we ask is permission to hold the meeting in the large patio next to the church. It will be a simple meeting. We will sing some songs and show the people that God can speak Tepehuan as well as Spanish, and afterward we will give out soda pop and cookies to all who come."

It was a bold request. Loreto, Narcisa and the handful of believers were barely tolerated by the community. While no believer at this point had suffered physical abuse, they did suffer the abuse of indifference, hate and ridicule. And the villagers had a derogatory name they called the believers behind their backs—*alleluias*.

But now the general stood up and used the term directly to Loreto's face.

"You are not one of us, Loreto. Your father was not Tepehuan and your Tepehuan mother abandoned you to be brought up by those who don't know our ways. Also, you and your wife are *alleluias* and we don't want such people in our community. Nor do we want the Book. Why should we want such a Book when none of us can read? Nor do we want the soda pop and cookies you will be passing out at your meeting. You might poison us. And if that *gringo* Burt comes back, we will hang him."

Loreto gave the general a respectful nod of his head, tipped his sombrero, turned and walked away. As soon as he was out of earshot, the general motioned for three of his council policemen. "That *alleluia* needs to know we mean what we say. We don't want him to have that special service in honor of that Book. See that he understands our minds."

Landlocked at 6,500 feet above sea level, Fig Tree Village sits in a small oval valley surrounded by stands of thick-trunked, sweet-smelling ponderosa pines. Most of the 600 inhabitants of the village are Mexican or mestizo and wrest a living in sawmill-related activities.

The Tepehuans, on the other hand, live in a kind of buffer zone on small farms or ranches around the village. There they plow the hard-packed ground with oxen and steel-tipped wooden plows just as their fathers did before them and their fathers before them. Until recent years, no one who hadn't hiked out the three days by mule to the mail town of Paral, had ever seen a truck. There is neither electricity, running water or paved streets in Fig Tree Village and the people's worldview is limited to a few news broadcasts and country western music picked up by transistor radio.

Following the true Tepehuan pattern, Loreto and Narcisa lived on a small ranch about two miles outside of town. As Loreto walked home that late afternoon, he wondered how he would break the news to Narcisa. After all, as a co-translator with the Bascoms, she more than he had been the one most responsible for the completion of the Tepehuan New Testament. As a young girl, she had found the Lord while working with Burt and his wife Marvel. And how would he explain the general's decision to the Bascoms? They were the ones who had written to ask him to arrange for the dedication service, and they, with other guests, would be arriving in just a few days.

It must have been these thoughts that blocked out the sound of footsteps behind him. Because from out of nowhere, Loreto suddenly felt rough hands grabbing at his neck, arms and legs. Instinctively, he new it was an ambush ordered by the general. More out of reflex reaction than bravery, he spun around in a wild effort to free himself from his attackers and tried to run. As he made his first bolt, he felt a stinging blow to his nose. Someone grabbed his shirt and then he felt a prick in his leg like a dog had bitten him. But no hands held him fast and he raced away from his assailants with the speed of a deer.

When Loreto entered his one-room, mud-walled house and saw Narcisa's walnut-colored cheeks flush with concern, he brushed aside the attack as inconsequential. "Just some ruffians trying to make a name for themselves by harrassing the Christians," he said. But when Narcisa pushed back her long black hair from her face and attended to Loreto's bloodied nose, she saw his torn shirt and the stab wound in his leg. She knew the attack was more serious than her husband would admit to her and the children.

Thus, a few days later when Wycliffe translator Dr. Burt Bascom and his wife Marvel and their guests flew into Fig Tree Village for the dedication, the tiny band of Christians was discouraged. Believing in and acting upon the biblical injunction to make amends quickly with one's adversaries, Burt, Loreto, and three American friends who had come for the dedication, decided to visit the general and once again ask his permission to hold the dedication in the patio next to the village church.

A light winter rain was falling when the pickup rolled into the general's yard. With the general was a large group of other Tepehuan men, all of whom had been drinking a volatile corn liquor.

"Come closer," said the general as Burt and the others climbed out of the pickup. Immediately, Burt strode to shake the general's hand. "I have come closer," said Burt. It was the typical Tepehuan greeting and the general seemed not at all surprised to see Burt or Loreto or the other men who had come to visit.

To escape the rain, the general invited the men up onto his front porch. There under the eaves of weatherworn ponderosa pine shakes, Burt parried the remarks of the general and the other Tepehuan men who had gathered around to laugh and field ribald jokes.

During a momentary lull in the laughter, Burt took out the recently published Tepehuan New Testament and asked if he might read from it. The general nodded his approval and Burt began to read from Romans 12:9. After reading the words, "really love each other," Burt paused and asked the general if these weren't good words. "They are good," said the general. After each of Paul's admonitions to "hate what is evil, to cling to what is good, to love one another," Burt paused and asked the same question, and each time the general agreed the words were good.

As Burt continued to read, he suddenly became aware that the men had become silent. They all reflected surprise and awe when they realized the words coming off the page were Tepehuan.

Moments later, Burt asked the general's grandson to read from the New Testament, and the same sense of astonishment struck the men as they responded with, "The Book talks Tepehuan! The Book talks Tepehuan!" Equally astounding, a Tepehuan man was the one who was reading!

Then just before Burt, Loreto and their friends excused themselves, Burt presented the general with a New Testament. "I've translated this Book for all Tepehuans," said Burt, "and on Sunday when the sun is half-way up the eastern portion of the sky, I would like to present the Book to the townspeople. To do this, I would like your permission to use the large patio next to the church."

Without a smile, the general said, "I'll let you know on Sunday."

Gently the early morning Sunday sun spilled its warmth and clear light into the frost-filled nooks and crannies of the brown valley. As the sun rose higher and higher toward the 10:30 hour, almost no one had arrived for the dedication. And those who were planning the celebration still hadn't heard from the general. But by midday, when the sun was at its zenith, a large crowd of Tepehuan people had gathered in and around the front yard of Peter and Mary Thiessen (workers with New Tribes Mission who were helping with the dedication service). Most of them had walked several hours for this occasion, but still no one knew exactly where the important event would take place.

When Burt received another "I'll let you know later" reply from the general, he decided to hold the service in the Thiessens' front yard. About 2 p.m., after a battery-operated loudspeaker had filled the mountain air with a variety of Christian hymns, the service began. Many of those assembled stood under the eaves of a large shed to escape the hot sun; others lounged on the wire fence or sat on scrap-lumber pine boards supported by chairs at either end. A guitar-strumming quartet provided the special music. Burt prayed, read from the New Testament, and in a short speech, reminded them why he had come to Fig Tree Village almost forty years before.

"When my wife Marvel and I first came here, I told you then we had come to learn the Tepehuan language. I said I wanted to learn your language because I wanted to write it down and make a book. Today I have brought you the Book."

After a few more songs, a short primer demonstration proved that anyone who could read Spanish could also learn to read Tepehuan. Narcisa and Loreto were re-

cognized as indispensable co-translators. Then, as
Marvel and the other expatriate guests helped serve a
light refreshment of soda pop and cookies, a few bought
New Testaments. And then the service was over.

Later, at a remote ranch cottage some distance from
the center of the dedication activity, Burt, and several
guests, paid a social call on Loreto and Narcisa
Herrera, the two people who had steadfastly worked on
the translation with Burt and Marvel.

As we sat together on rough, handmade stools that
rested on the uneven, hard-packed dirt of their front
porch, Narcisa reflected on how God had ministered to
her as she worked on the New Testament. As this small,
plain woman began to speak, the reality of the completed
Tepehuan New Testament broke over her, and she wept
openly and unashamedly. So did Burt. Through her
tears, she told how a few months earlier the small group
of believers had prayed for her and God had healed her
from a serious sickness.* In fact, it was such a remarkable healing that unbelieving neighbors, who had seen
her the evening before, were startled to see her up and
ministering to her faimily. "Narcisa," they said, "you
were almost dead yesterday, and now look at you. You
are up and well!" Translating the many stories in the
New Testament where Jesus had healed the sick had
impressed Narcisa and the other believers that God
still heals.

One of the visitors asked Narcisa why, in the face of
indifference, ridicule and hostility, she and her husband
had continued to faithfully translate for so many years.
"I continued on," she said, "because I believe we were
chosen to do this work. This Book is important. Our
people, and all people everywhere, need to know there

*See letter at the end of the chapter.

is a good road to follow. I want everyone to know as I do
that they can be in Jesus Christ and when they die they
will go to be with Him."

"Narcisa," I said, "you don't have a lot of money; you
don't have a large house or car, and you don't have the
power of rich people. But I want you to know that you
are noble in the sight of God. God is honored and
pleased because you have chosen the Pearl of Great
Price. You have great treasure waiting for you in
heaven!"

As I left the little house set up against the purple
mountains with the wind whispering around the pine-
shake eaves, I tried to interpret the immediate significance of the dedication of the Tepehuan New Testament.
A large number of people now understood that, with a
little effort, they could learn to read and understand the
meaning of words they read. Contrary to some who
belittled their speech, they finally knew their language
was a "real" language. They had a book to prove it! It
was also remarkable to realize that Narcisa and Loreto
had remained loyal to Jesus Christ in the face of
extreme censorship, social embarrassment and harrass-
ment. I thought about Burt and Marvel's high resolve
and courage to willingly give forty years of their lives to
this community of people isolated from the mainstream
of society. Because they had been willing to go and
others had been willing to give and pray, this community,
steeped in hostility and outspokenness against right-
eousness, had received the Seed, the Truth, a Book that
actually spoke Tepehuan, a Book that had power to
bring about spiritual change.

* * * * *

Marvel and Burt,

Very esteemed friends,

It is with real pleasure that I write this letter to greet you and to wish you good health. We here are all in good health thanks to our Lord Who loves us so very much. Many people have seen the great power which our God has demonstrated in me. I don't know what I ought to do. What does He want with me?

I really wasn't afraid to die, but I kept thinking of my family. Who knows what they would have done, but God loves them very much, just as you do. I don't know how to repay you for having helped me at just the right time. The doctors said I was toxic from so much medication.

When we left Baborigame [and landed in Parral] we went from the landing field to the doctor's house, and he himself took us in his car to [the hospital in] El Valle. They took me in immediately and examined me and took an X-ray. The first thing they told me was that I had an infection in my right lung. They gave me a shot and while the doctors were in consultation I lay down in the hallway on my blanket.

Finally they told us we'd have to go to a specialist in Chihuahua, but that the ambulance was very busy. So Loreto decided to hire a taxi to make the round trip [4 hours one way]. While Loreto was making arrangements for the taxi, a doctor was ready. They did some tests which they were unable to do in El Valle—or rather they didn't have the equipment for the tests.

That same night we returned to El Valle. They didn't put me in the hospital there. [I needed] lots of liquids. We got a room in a lady's house. Everyone was very kind to us—thanks to God. Very quickly I recovered a little bit. I just needed rest and losts of liquids. Now I am much better—a bit weak, but I am with my children. The third of June we have to return for more tests. They say they will evaluate my condition. But I don't understand what that means.

I haven't talked to Gregorio to find out if you left me a copy of the dictionary—I want to see it. If you didn't leave anything, please send me one because I can look it over. I can't do heavy work.

Every day I've been spending time reading the New Testament from the Tepehuan translation [and translating it] into Spanish for the children because many things they did not understand. But I don't think there's another New Testament as simple as the Tepehuan New Testament.

I really appreciate all our brothers and sisters in Christ who have been concerned about my health, and for the money they have sent. Also for the prayers of others. The Lord has answered demonstrating his love for my family. Every day I am reminded that God really loves them very much—that's why He allows me to remain with them because they were sad when I was so sick.

Narcisa

— 7 —

The Tyranny of Indifference

I sat on a Dutch colonial balcony in Suriname, South America and watched fireflies splash dots of white over banana trees silhouetted in the garden below. The tropical night was alive with the sounds of crickets, tree toads and the chortle of night birds and indistinguishable mammals.

But the sound that occupied my mind as I sat in a woven wicker chair in the darkness of that humid tropical night was not the distant cry of a howler monkey or a three-foot kinkajou squealing over its kill. The sound that filled my mind was that of a broken man's spirit, of disillusionment, of shattered dignity and aspiration, The sound was the lamentation of a man who had given up on life and taken refuge in drink.

His name was Fred. I had met him when I changed planes on a flight from Mexico to San Juan, Puerto Rico and on to Port of Spain, Trinidad. I was on my way to Brazil via Mexico and Suriname to gather material for what was later to become the book *To the Ends of the Earth*.[4]

With no direct flights from Los Angeles and flight schedules limited to one a week, Suriname is truly one of those places where "you can't get there from here." However, it was precisely this remote little-known country with its sides bulging into Guyana on the west and French Guyana on the east that activated my spirit of adventure. Of course, if SIL hadn't had several linguistic, literacy, support and Bible translation teams working there, I probably would have flown directly to Brazil. I have a particular aversion to long flights that involve several touchdown stops, and as in this case, a twenty-four hour delay in Port of Spain, Trinidad.

If it weren't that long flights afford me a wonderful uninterrupted time to read (I usually carry four or five books—mostly Christian apologetics), I would be happy never to fly again. Jamming my six-foot-two-inch, two-hundred-pounds-plus frame into the narrow airplane seats for ten to twelve hours is something I can happily do without!

Compounding my discomfort on this flight was the unsettling reality that I had contracted Montezuma's Revenge. I was paying the price for my indiscriminate eating habits during my stopover in Mexico.

So now here I was, sitting in anonymity next to the window, buckling myself in after rushing through an unfamiliar airport and just barely making my connections. After such encounters with Montezuma, I've learned that if I keep myself perfectly still and look neither to the left nor to the right, I can sometimes foil the Revenge from attacking at will.

I was nicely strapped in with my head tilted back when Fred, who soon introduced himself, sat down next to me in the aisle seat. He was a bespectacled man, slender, in his early fifties, yet with skin that was clear and soft and free of the normal vicissitudes of aging. I nodded weakly and returned the introduction. And that was that. The plane took off for Port of Spain with intermediate stops in Guadeloupe and Grenada.

It was a congenial flight. The steady hum of the plane's big jet engines mixed with the passengers' lighthearted conversation created a soothing aura of confidence and goodwill. The flight attendants were vivacious, attentive and smiled easily as they passed out vacuum-sealed packets of salted almonds and took requests for drinks.

Like most of the passengers, Fred reflected a casual, easygoing attitude. I noticed, however, his drinks were always alcoholic and wondered how much of his easygoing nature was supported by something other than his natural disposition.

When we landed at St. George's, Grenada, Fred deplaned along with a number of the other passengers. I remained on board, still believing firmly that inactivity was the best insurance against further revenge by Montezuma. When he returned, Fred was all smiles. "Best place to buy rum," he said proudly.

We were soon airborne and the queasiness in my stomach left me long enough to accept the evening meal and to learn something about my traveling companion.

For reasons unexplained, Fred had left the United States in the mid-fifties to find his fortune in the West Indies. "I spent a couple of months living on several of the islands, including Curacao, Trinidad and Tobago," he said. "I opted for Grenada." (He had since moved to another island.) I learned that Fred opened a general store, married and raised three daughters and that his wife taught school (without pay) and finally became the headmistress.

As he talked, I felt a certain warmth toward him. He was free of arrogance or pretense. He smiled and laughed easily, but I sensed a deep inner sadness. He seemed well-read and was well-versed in world affairs.

As we neared Port of Spain, I asked if he could recommend the name of a decent hotel. "There's a guest house near the airport," he said. "In fact, I am going there myself. We can share a taxi."

"Thank you," I said. "That will be great."

When he learned my plane for Suriname wasn't leaving until 7:00 p.m. the following day, he suggested I spend the day with a good-looking girl. "Thanks," I said. "It's not my style."

By the time we cleared customs, found a cab and checked into the guest house, it was about 9:30 or 10:00 p.m. The guest house had a delicious-looking pool all brightly lit with multi-colored lights. I love to swim and after such a long, cramped flight, nothing seemed more appealing than a quiet night swim in a tropical pool. But my stomach wouldn't cooperate. Instead, I headed for the bar—the only place I could find that might have a Seven-Up or ginger ale to settle my stomach.

The bar was almost empty except for a couple of people talking softly at a table near the open patio. I had made my purchase and already headed back to my room when I met Fred. "Aha!" he said. "I see you've found the most important room in the house." We exchanged a few remarks and then he said, "Would you come back to my room for a drink?" It was late, I was tired, my stomach was upset, but I saw something in his eyes—that deep sadness—I had noticed on the plane.

"Okay," I said. "I'll take my Seven-Up and visit a bit."

On his nightstand lay a Gideon Bible; next to that, a large bottle of rum. Fred set down the Coke he had purchased at the bar, picked up the bottle of rum and began unsuccessfully to open it.

I sat opposite him on one of the two single beds in his room and watched. His teeth were clenched with determination, but his motor skills that would normally coordinate his hands were dulled by the large amount of alcohol he had already consumed. In the midst of his fumbling with the jug's fasteners, he said confidently, "I've never yet seen a bottle I couldn't get into."

Determination finally paid off. Fred conquered the problem of the jug's fasteners and poured out the golden liquid into a glass containing Coke and water.

"Why do you do this?" My voice was firm, but kind. Again I asked, "Why...why do you do this?" In retrospect I think my approach might have been wrong. The impulse to change comes from being loved rather than from being challenged. But in this case, Fred didn't react as if I had challenged him. He simply looked thoughtful, took a sip of his drink, looked down while he fondled his glass and said, "It makes me sleepy, and it makes me feel good. I never bother anyone; I keep to myself. I believe in living and let live. I keep to myself and it's not hurting anyone."

"It's hurting you," I said. "What about your liver?"

"I had a mild stroke two years ago. The doctor said it was due to . . ." Fred didn't finish his sentence. "If I get liver problems, I guess I'll quit—if I can. I suppose it's a kind of escape."

"Do you ever go to church?" I asked.

"I did as a child," said Fred. "I outgrew it. Church turns me off." I wasn't surprised with his answer. His response to the Bible was also predictable. "The Scriptures need to be interpreted. There are contradictions."

As I sat listening to Fred, I realized it was no accident that I was at that moment sitting across the bed from him. It was clear in my mind that God had indeed led me to him. Thus I felt the weight of 1 Peter 3:15, "Always be prepared to give an answer to everyone who asks you to give the reason for the hope that you have" (NIV).

Strictly speaking, Fred hadn't asked me anything— only that I keep him company. At that moment, I began to think about who I was. I had given (at that moment) twenty years of my life to an organization that had as its primary objective the longing to reach out to ethnic peoples with the Good News of Jesus Christ through the agency of translated Scriptures. Many of these were the poor, underprivileged and unevangelized. Fred was not an ethnic minority, he wasn't materially poor and he wasn't totally unevangelized (he often listened to radio preachers). But just as surely as any ethnic minority without the Scriptures in their own language, Fred needed to know that God's love and grace could release him from the tyranny of himself. How could I get through to him?

"You talk about love. I've been trying to find the meaning of that word all my life." he said. "I've looked for answers to life in all sorts of places. In fact I just finished reading Eric Fromm's book *The Art of Loving.* [5] And I still don't know the meaning of love."

"The Bible is the basis for all we know about love and about God," I said. "That's where you will find the answers you are looking for." And so we talked at length about God's sacrificial demonstration of love as seen in Jesus Christ.

For a while, we switched the subject and Fred told me
something more about his life on the islands. During
Grenada's independence, Fred's store was looted—
even by his employees. His insurance only paid half the
losses. Later he was robbed and mugged in his own bed.
It was only by playing dead, he said, that his assailants
left him alone. At that point, Fred decided to leave the
Islands and return to the United States. (That's where
he was coming from on this trip. He had a small farm in
North Carolina.) "That's been the story of my life," he
said, "almost, but not quite making it. And I don't see
why I should bother God about my problems."

"How do you feel when your children treat you with
indifference?" I said.

Fred lowered his head. "It makes me sad," he said.

"That's exactly the way God feels when we treat Him
with indifference. God stands with his arms wide open
and says, 'Fred, I love you. I showed you how much I
loved you when I sent my Son Jesus to die in your place
and pay for your sins.' When I learned that God loved
me with such intensity and passion, then I wanted to
return that love by obeying Him. I learned how He
wanted me to live by reading the Bible and by modeling
my life after his Son Jesus Christ. That's what it means
to have a personal relationship with God through
Christ.

"You told me your daughters are often upset with
you; that they are ashamed of your drinking. Let me tell
you something. You are valuable to God. He loves and
cares for you. He thinks you are important."

Fred smiled wistfully. "No one has told me that in
twenty years."

To my surprise, he reached back into his battered
suitcase and pulled out a Living New Testament. "A

woman friend of mine asked me to bring her a copy. Is this a good Bible to read?"

"It is indeed," I said. "Just like this one on your nightstand. Would you like me to read some passages for you?"

Fred nodded and handed me the Bible. Earlier, he had made some comment that nowhere did the Bible speak about the necessity of people caring for one another. I read a passage from Romans, chapter 12 where Paul asks the Christians to love each other with brotherly affection and that the believers ought to get into the habit of inviting guests home for dinner.

It was now just past midnight and we were both getting sleepy. I suggested he read for himself some of the earlier chapters of Romans and John's Gospel I had already paraphrased. Then I told him that I had written a book called *Manuel,*[6] about a young man who had found meaning and fulfillment in his life through a personal faith and trust in Jesus Christ. "The book is back in my room," I said, "but I will go and get it if you will read it." He said he would.

When I returned to Fred's room, he was stretched out on his bed listening to some radio preacher. I handed him the book. Inside I had written: "To Fred. Jesus really does love you! John 15:9-14. ('Greater love has no one than this, that he lay down his life for his friends'— Living Bible.) That's how much Jesus loves you."

Fred saw me to the door and shook my hand. "Tell me," he said, "what do you think about radio preachers?" He then named one who spent most of his program time asking for money and calling down communism.

"Some are very good," I said. "Others like this have forgotten their true purpose and reason for being. They are probably cultish."

Fred smiled. "There's hope for you yet," he said.

"There is hope for you, too," I said. "I'll be praying that you will discover the true meaning of love."

I thought about Fred all during my time in Suriname. I couldn't help but contrast Fred with a twenty-two-year-old man I learned about from Wycliffe translator Naomi Glock who works with the Saramaccan people in Suriname.

"The Saramaccans have never had a serious understanding of what it means to have a new life in Jesus Christ," she said. "But two years ago, Samo, a twenty-two-year-old Saramaccan man who helps my partner Catherine Rountree and me translate, accepted Jesus Christ into his life. A short time later his mother died and when it came time for the funeral, he refused to take part in anything that had to do with prayers or offerings to the spirits.

"The Saramaccans have more than thirty different spirits which they call *kooms*, most of whom are terrifying avenging spirits and must be placated with offerings and prayers and by observing certain taboos. Samo, however, with great courage and faith said, 'No. I have found the true God of heaven and earth. It is He Who is stronger than all *kooms*.' At that point, other people began to sit up and take notice. Never had anyone ever questioned or stood against the dreaded *kooms*.

"As the weeks passed, the people of the village noticed Samo was still alive, still their friend, and continued firmly to resist all contact with the spirits.

"One day a man came to Samo and told him he was impressed that his garden was growing even though he knew Samo had not asked the *kooms* to bless it. "I like what you are and the freedom you have,' said the man, 'but I don't believe I could be a Saramaccan and a Christian at the same time.'

"Samo assured him he could and explained how he himself had become a Christian. Shortly after that, this man and four others accepted the Lord Jesus Christ— the true God of heaven and earth, the One Who is stronger than all *kooms*."

It was late when I finally got up from my wicker chair on that Dutch colonial balcony. It was my last night in Suriname. I would be flying to Brazil the following afternoon. I thought about Fred and Samo. Fred didn't know it (or did he?) but he, like the Saramaccan people, was controlled by a dark spirit as terrifying as any of the *kooms*. I prayed that night for Fred. (Later I wrote him and sent him some other books.) I prayed that like Samo, Fred, in Christ's strength, would find the personal freedom in the One Who is stronger than all the dreaded *kooms* of the universe.

One of Satan's dark tricks of tyranny is to lull Western man into a certain smug indifference; to trick him into being satisfied with letting life and life's experiences be the highest moral authority. The reality of such a posture is no true peace, no true satisfaction, no true excitement. Fred and all the other Freds in the world believe their drinking isn't harming anyone. In actuality their indifference robs themselves, their families and their world of men fully alive, imbued with the spirit of life. Samo, on the other hand, by faith in Jesus Christ, had the courage to shuck off his dark spirit. The result was a discovered secret, a secret known only to those who begin to take God seriously and enter into a

union of divine love in which the captive heart and life
are set eternally free.

The thief comes only to steal and to kill and destroy;
I have come that they may have life and have it to the full
(John 10:10 NIV).

— 8 —

The Promotion
of a Servant-Warrior

I opened the door of the convalescent hospital and stepped inside. Two nurses sat with the receptionist. It was Monday noon, and over their salads, sandwiches and conversation, a nurse looked up and asked if she could help me.

"I'm here to see Lulu Reber," I said.

"Straight ahead, and it's the first door on the right."

I smiled my thanks, turned on my heel and took the first of my yard-long strides toward the corridor. But before I picked up speed, the nurse stopped me with, "Have you seen Lu recently?"

"No, not for several weeks," I said.

"You'll see a great change. She's deteriorated greatly in the last few days. Be prepared."

It was a three-bed ward. In the bed nearest the window, a woman with thin chalk-white hair slept curled up in the fetal position. The middle bed was empty, and Lu Reber occupied the bed nearest the door.

I expected Lu to be alone, but sitting beside her in a most loving way was Helen Ashdown—friend and colleague from the days when Lu had worked in Mexico. (Actually, Helen was spelling off Jeanne Lindholm who had provided almost constant care and vigilance since Lu first took sick.)

I had seen people on their deathbeds before, but when I looked at the person before me, I asked Helen, "Is this Lu?"

Helen smiled weakly and softly said, "Yes."

I laid my hand on Lu's forehead. Her skin was like wax—cold and lifeless. What monstrous disease is this cancer? A few weeks before she had almost been her old self—a salty warrior who spoke with the harsh accent of her native Philadelphia, an accent she hadn't lost in all her seventy-plus years. Now she was slipping in and out of a coma, eyes like glass, fretful movements. Even with my limited medical experience, I knew the end, or more correctly, the promotion was at hand.

"Hi," I said cheerfully.

"Do you know Hugh?" asked Helen.

There was a slight movement of Lu's head, but that was all. Then Helen and I talked, and as we talked, I remembered the first time I met this old warrior. It was June 1957.

Lu, Jim Walker, a Wycliffe colleague, myself and Neil McKay, a friend from my hometown of Vancouver, Canada, took a canoe trip through the swamps of Tabasco. Our destination was Ash, an isolated Chontal village where we were to distribute some pamphlets printed in the Chontal language describing the government's plan to stamp out malaria.

The trip into the state of Tabasco had been most interesting. At one point, a raft ferrying my car across a small river broke loose just as the front wheels touched the riverbank. I thought the car and I were going for a swim! But what I remember most about that trip was not the mud, the heat, the turtle stew or an all-night village fiesta. What I remember most was Lu Reber washing out my socks and muddy tennis shoes.

When we arrived at Ash, I jumped out of the canoe and fell into a mud hole. I left my socks on the edge of the canoe to dry while we went to deliver the pamphlets around the village. When we returned, there was Lu, who had walked on ahead, washing out the mud from my socks. And then she insisted on washing my shoes as well! Just a little thing, you say. Hardly worth writing about. Yet in that selfless act, Lu demonstrated her true character—the character of a servant. It was this that characterized her whole life and ministry.

As I thought about that incident, I couldn't help but hear the words of our Lord when He said, "Whoever wants to become great among you must be your servant; and whoever wants to be first must be your slave" (Matthew 20:26-27 NIV).

After faithfully serving in various positions in Mexico, including secretary to the late John Beekman, she served with great distinction during the last several years of her life in the Huntington Beach mail room. It was true that Lu was occasionally abrasive with little tolerance for those who didn't work as long or as hard or as conscientiously as she thought they should. But behind that rough exterior was indeed the heart of a servant—a servant who knew what the word "commitment" was all about.

Lu was not only a committed servant but a giving servant. Many of our Wycliffe family were the recipients of a small gift of money in an envelope, or a treat, or flowers on a special day from this generous servant heart.

And in that diminutive body also beat the heart of a warrior. I chose this word carefully because warrior

means more than fighter. Warrior also means volunteer,
enlisted person, rank and file, veteran and standard
bearer.

This is how Lu Reber lived her three score and ten
and I am confident that on the day she entered into that
greater life, the Lord, with a smile said:

*Well done, good and faithful servant. You have
been faithful with a few things; I will put you in
charge of many things. Come and share your
master's happiness (Matthew 25:21 NIV).*

— 9 —

Grabbing Hold
of the Word of God

My flight out of Saigon (now Ho Chi Minh City) was delayed four hours. It was 1972 and one of the most decisive battles of the war had just been fought at An Loc. (I would have to return home to read my *Time* magazine to discover just how decisive!) The Saigon airport bubbled with confusion, mild hysteria, military and national news media. I was in the middle of a six-week assignment to gather data and take photos for two book projects. One became *Language and Faith;*[7] the other, *Joy of a Loving Jonathan* (later combined into the book *It Takes Time to Love*).[8]

When I finally arrived in Manila, I had just enough time for a quick shower before dinner with my colleagues at the SIL group house on the city's outskirts. Afterward, around 8:00 p.m., I retired for a few hours' sleep before getting up at 12:00 midnight to catch what was known locally as the "Red Eye Special"—a flight that left Manila at 3:00 a.m. for Mindanao in the south. It had been hot in Saigon, but Manila was like a Turkish steam bath, and I slept fitfully until I was awakened by the driver who was to take me to the airport.

To my chagrin, I discovered that both the driver and I had overslept. To this day, I don't know how he sped through those narrow streets, across intersections and around blind corners as if there were no other cars in the city. I have never been a white-knuckle passenger, but that night I'm sure I would have been if I'd had the nerve to look out the window!

I reached the airport and scrambled up the stairs to board the aircraft (no security in those days) just as the flight attendant was getting ready to secure the door.

After getting settled and calming myself, I spoke with one of the flight attendants. As we talked, I discovered he and I had a mutual friend living in Canada, the son of the then-Philippine Consul General. As a gesture of friendship, he invited me up to the flight deck to watch the sun rise. It was as beautiful a sight as I have ever seen. Clusters of miniature islands were set like jewels in a sparkling azure sea, all glistening in the wash of a brilliant morning sun.

As we talked, my new friend asked the inevitable. "Why have you come to the Philippines? What do you do for a living?"

Sometimes this is an easy question to answer. "I write historical biographies," I say. Or, "I write true-life adventure stories." Or, "I write stories about people whose lives and motives are in transition; who are undergoing a spiritual metamorphosis as they reevaluate themselves and their values in light of the New Testament Scriptures."

The latter is a dangerous and threatening answer to most. Even if I modify it, the response is generally, "Oh, isn't that interesting!" Or, "That's nice." and then silence. Often what was before a genuinely warm and friendly conversation, turns suddenly cold and frequently indifferent. One man on a flight from Accra in West Africa to Tamale in the north had taken the initiative in our conversation. He was more than willing to answer a young man's first-time-visit questions about Africa. But when he learned that my motivations and those of the organization I represented were spiritual as well as scientific and humanitarian, he buried his head in his newspaper. He was now beyond the reach of meaningful conversation. I didn't want this to happen to my new friend, the flight attendant.

"I am a writer," I said. "I work with people who are highly motivated and committed to giving the New Testament Scriptures to ethnic peoples who as yet don't have them available in their language. Since the Philippines has over 150 different languages, my organization, The Summer Institute of Linguistics, has people working with a large number of ethnic peoples here. Part of my job is to write about how some of these people respond to the New Testament Scriptures as they begin to apply them to their daily lives."

I don't remember with accuracy what the flight attendant said. But I remember well how another attendant who was listening to this conversation responded. "It must by terribly dull to spend all your time writing," she said.

I returned to my seat shaking my head. The writing, I thought, is hard. It's painful, exasperating, mind-boggling, frightening, always solitary, but never dull. How can it be dull when you have the privilege of writing about people who have confronted the Living God and accepted his offer of love, grace and eternal life through faith in his Son, Jesus Christ? How can it be dull to walk into the lives of people who have been given new gifts of spirituality, vitality, a new wholeness and boldness about themselves and the way they live and view their lives? How can it be dull to watch the dazzling reality dawn in a person's mind and heart that their personal commitment to Christ means they have God's promise that death, the enemy of all hope, is destroyed in Jesus Christ?

Over the years, I have interviewed scores of people who have spoken happily about a new reality and direction in their lives; how this has come about through the freshly translated New Testament Scriptures in their own language. Many who, while not using this terminology, have told me of being born again by the Spirit of God.

I met some of them in 1967 when I spent five days between Christmas and New Year's visiting my dear friends and colleagues, Dr. Calvin Rensch and his wife Carolyn in the village of Arroyo Tomate (Tomato Gulch) in southern Mexico. This was one of my first "official" trips as writer and photographer for Wycliffe. The results of that trip were several published articles and a series of remarkable tape-recorded interviews that have lain, until this moment, unused and unread. I kept pushing them aside in favor of more "urgent" projects. Now with this anthology, I am pleased to present the candid, radiantly triumphant testimonies of four Chinantec men as they encountered the Living God.

* * * * *

My name is Peter and I live in Tomato Gulch. You asked me to tell you how I felt when I first heard about the God Who is alive. My reaction at first was both happy and sad. When I thought about how many sorrows came to us when we worshipped idols, I was sad. But I was glad when I heard that anyone could speak to the Living God whenever and wherever he wanted. When I first began to hear about these things, I said to my friends, "Oh, do you suppose these words from the paper could truly be the words of God?" My friends said, "Yes, they are." They urged me to go and listen when the words from the paper were read. I did. I knew I had sinned and was happy to learn that when we believe in the Living God, our sins are forgiven.

But then I was sad because at first I didn't think it would be possible for me to learn to read the paper that told me about this Living God. I had tried to read many times, even spending all day, but there were always places I didn't understand. So I decided to fast and pray. I thought then I would be able to learn to read.

When I was learning to read, the authorities in Tomato Gulch gave me great sorrow. They said, "See what an example the old man is giving his son." They were talking about me and my desire to learn to read and *grab hold of the Word* [Chinantec idiom for becoming a believer in Christ].

Then the time came when I was learning to read with great understanding. For this I was put in jail. But I was determined to keep on learning to read. In fact, I said to myself, "Because of this great sorrow, I am going to apply myself even more diligently. Those who have thrown me in jail would just love it if I would give up the Word of God, but I will not."

I must tell you also that even though they gave me great sorrow, I was not afraid of my jailers.

I was finally released, but a second time they put me in jail. There were four others who had also grabbed hold of the Word, and they slept, but not me. I didn't sleep a wink all night. I just talked constantly to God.

There were people standing and talking in the doorway of the jail. They kept saying, "Now there is a person who will escape." They said this because I didn't sleep. None of us wanted to escape even though they kept us for four days.

On the fourth day, they let us out and the elders of the village said, "Let this teach you a lesson. Now others know what happens when the traditions of our people aren't followed. You have been disgraced. No one will listen to you now." But the elders were wrong. When they put us in jail, God caused us to multiply.

First of all we spoke to God. We asked Him that we would become more numerous. We asked that there would be those of our brethren who would pay attention to the Word of God. We made it our business to learn more and more about what the Word of God said on the paper [The Gospel of Mark]. Every afternoon we went from house to house. And now we thank God very much that He gave us more and more brethren who grabbed hold of the Word.

After we came out of jail, God caused us to become twelve in number. As I speak, we number over three hundred. Now I, Pete, will stop talking. I will let my son Gregory continue the story.

* * * * *

This is Gregory speaking. I want to tell you how we came to build the church. It seemed very beautiful, the way we all met every afternoon, going from house to house. Then one day, those of us who were listening to the Word of God, made an agreement that we would build a house where all of us could meet together and where others could become brethren [Christians].

It was our idea that if we met in such a place, other people would come. We thought they would be less embarrassed to listen to the Word of God in a house that didn't belong to a person.

We asked all of our fellow men if they were willing for such a project to take place. They said they were. Even those who had come close to grabbing hold of the Word of God said they would help.

They were all glad for such a house and many of those who were close to grabbing hold of the Word of God came to be brethren when the house was finished. But those people whose heart had not changed, saw the brethren were becoming more numerous, and they became angry. They spoke badly about us and spread false stories telling others we were bad and that what we were doing was an evil thing.

But that didn't stop us. With joy we worked on the church building. Each of the brethren contributed what he could. Some brought leaves for thatching the roof. Some made benches. In this way we didn't have to stand to listen to the Word of God. This was a good thing. When we didn't have benches, some got peevish when they had to stand for a long time listening to the Word of God!

* * * * *

My name is Octave. I would like to tell you the way it was for me in the past. I used to think fiestas were very important. We believed anyone who played in the band to honor the images would be right in God's eyes. Being a musician in our culture is a religious experience.

One day I met one of the brothers who said, "Let's go listen to the Word of God this afternoon."

"All right," I said, "but where will this be?"

"At the house of the brother who has come from far away," he said.

I said, with some skepticism, "Is there really and truly a Word of God?"

"Yes," he said, "there really is." So, believing him, I went to hear what was written on the paper. As I listened, I thought, "Is this really true? Do you suppose there really is a Living God? Is it right that the images we worship aren't really living?"

For several days I thought about these things. Each afternoon I listened to the glad news of God from the paper. As I listened I slowly came to believe and know that truly, truly this that I was hearing was the Word of God.

When our brother who gave us the paper—the one who came from far away—said, the reason Jesus came to earth was to take off my sins and to save me, I thought clearly about what he said. I said to my wife, "Do you want to grab hold of the Word of God?"

"Yes, yes," she said. "If it is true that there is a Word of God, I, like you, want to have it."

In this way we both grabbed hold of the Word of God. We were happy that Jesus had come to take off our sins.

Some time later, great sorrow came to our household. My wife became very sick. It looked as if she might die. We prayed and read the paper [Gospel of Mark]. And we asked others who had grabbed hold of the Word of God to also pray, and they did. The day finally came when my wife got well. Now she believes even stronger that God is great. We thank God that she was able to get well little by little. We are together until this day and are very happy.

* * * * *

Peter and Gregory and Octave have spoken. Now I, Barnabas, would like to speak. I want to tell you that when I was a little boy I wanted to do what God wanted. And like Octave, I thought the way to God was to become a musician and play for the fiestas that honor the images.

For seven years I played in the band for all our religious fiestas. I regarded the images highly. The elders would say [referring to the images], "Here is the Lord," and I believed them. But then I began to really look at the images. I noticed their arms and their eyes never moved. They were always in the same position. In this way, I came to believe the images were not alive.

It was about this time that I began to hear about the brother who had come from far away and about the paper on which was written the Word of God. One Sunday afternoon, I went over to this brother's house. There I saw four of our brethren in the house and they were reading from the paper. I became very happy and glad in my heart when I heard what the Gospel of Mark said. But like my brother Peter, I too became sad because I didn't know how to read.

I spoke to my brother who had come from far away. "Do you suppose I will ever learn to read?" I was startled by his answer. "You will learn to read very fast," he said.

Since my brother from far away said I could learn to read, I applied myself to learning how to read. It required studying many chapters of the paper. And finally when I did learn to read, there were many brethren.

But at the time when I was first learning, there were only six of us who had grabbed hold of the Word of God. And it was at that time the elders of the village began to make a fuss. They told us we were not doing and speaking the right things.

But all six of us were of one accord and we did everything together. And the more the people made a fuss, the more we applied ourselves to the Word of God. One day, when the elders and the people of the town made a fuss at us, we stood before all the people of the town and said, "We have accepted the Word of God. But is it right after we have spent money on the instruments to stop playing in the band? We are willing to play for the school fiestas, but we cannot play for the fiestas that honor the images. This we have decided because that is what the law of God says." This we told to all the townspeople.

The people were very angry and pointed their fingers at us. "Where do you think you have come from to know so much?" they shouted. "How have you suddenly become so very learned? Have you been up to heaven to see what it is like and now you have come back down to teach us, your elders?" And they laughed at us and called us many names.

These were hard words to hear. But because we did what God wanted us to do, our hearts were strengthened all the more. Yes, we did what God wanted us to do and we spoke to God in prayer and our hearts were very happy because we had grabbed hold of the Word of God.

* * * * *

When the first Chinantec believers encountered the translated Gospel of Mark, they recognized Jesus Christ as the One Who offered them Living Water that would slack their thirst for God; the One Who gave them joy because they were accepted by the Living God, their sins were forgiven and they had eternal life. But while the introduction of the Word of God brought gladness, it also brought persecutions and sufferings.

The first believers were jeered at, jailed and forbidden to use the main trails in and out of the village. Some were expelled from their homes and villages. In an effort to discourage their meeting together for prayer and fellowship around the Word, their church building was burned to the ground.

With this persecution came the temptation, as Jesus said in the parable of the Sower, for some seed to be snatched away, choked and left to wither and die. But Jesus also promised that some seed would take root and produce a crop of thirty, or sixty or even a hundred times what was sown (Mark 4:20). That's exactly what has happened to the Church in Tomato Gulch.

Nineteen years after they first began to live and work among the Chinantecs, Cal and Carolyn Rensch, with their co-workers, Bob and Jan Mugele who joined them in 1970, took part in the Chinantec New Testament dedication.

Said Cal, "When Carolyn and I went to the Chinantecs in 1956, we wondered how long it would be before we would see Chinantec Christian leaders publicly praising God for what He had done in their lives. At the dedication we saw this come to pass. For over an hour, leaders from thirty-four congregations in thirty towns spoke of God's working in their midst—all this in an atmosphere of political unrest and violence, even up to the time of the dedication."

But when the day came, more than 2,000 Chinantecs came to celebrate. Even some of the non-believers sent food for the occasion. In a town that had expelled the believers, eight New Testaments were sold. There were repeated evidences of how highly the people regarded the New Testament. One man who was bedridden, sent his wife a whole day's journey to buy a New Testament for himself and his brother. The arrival of the New Testament also worked in the hearts of some who had not been following the Word as fully as they knew they should.

Fearing there wouldn't be enough New Testaments to go around, the church elders limited the purchases to one New Testament per household. Seven hundred were sold that first day!

So important was this New Testament dedication that the elders had a new cement rostrum built in the church with the following words inscribed at its base:

On the twenty-third day of the month of February 1975, they gave thanks to God that the New Testament had been completed.

One of the first believers, Coconut Hill Louie, spoke for everyone when he said, "Before when I heard Spanish spoken in the church, I did not know what it was all about. I was in the dark. Before, I walked on evil paths and I fell in rough places. I didn't know what road to take. But all that has changed. We now have the glad news of God that shows me the road so much better. We thank God who gave us his Son. I talk to the Father God in heaven both day and night and thank Him that his Word is written down on paper!"

— 10 —

Data Incomplete

Have you ever flown in a helicopter before?" he asked.

"Yes," I said, "but never without the doors."

"I thought you would be able to get clearer pictures without shooting through a Plexi-glass door. Besides, it's a whole lot cooler in this bubble without the doors."

Wycliffe Bible Translators' Jungle Aviation and Radio Service (JAARS) pilot Jerry Ferguson was helping me get strapped into a three-seater Hiller Helicopter in Irian Jaya. I was on a photo and writing assignment in Indonesia and was about to take off on a twenty-minute flight to visit a group of people called the Bauzi.

I had just met Jerry and found him warm, friendly and eager to serve. I appreciated his sensitivity to my needs. Shooting photos free of the glare of a Plexi-glas door would give me both clearer and brighter photos, and even though I was strapped in, greater flexibility and movement in shooting.

I had learned earlier that the Bauzi people practice a traditional semi-nomadic hunting and gathering life-style. To maintain their lifestyle, the Bauzi live in tiny village clusters of about fifty people in remote parts of the jungle. What I didn't know was just how remote.

Shortly after lift-off in the helicopter, Jerry began to point out the direction of our flight on the charts resting in his lap. He had outfitted me with a radio headset in order to hear him over the roar of the helicopter's rotors.

Jungle flying is very much like flying over a vast ocean. Only, instead of water, there are trees—great endless carpets of trees that stretch to all four horizons. As I followed Jerry's flight path on the charts, I noticed there were elevations of mountains, rivers and other navigational aids. But as we moved closer and closer to the top side of the chart, I noticed a large white section without any such navigational aids. The only markings were the disquieting words: "Data incomplete" (information unreliable). We were flying into totally unexplored and uncharted "seas!"

Jerry had been to the Bauzis before, of course, and guided us safely to our destination, in spite of less-than-perfect navigational information. As we touched down on a grassy helicopter pad, I realized that if I had to reach this place by land or river travel, it probably would have taken five or six long, hard, exhausting and very dangerous days. When I met the translators to the Bauzi people, Dave and Joyce Briley, I thought how wonderful it was for them to have a skilled and dedicated JAARS pilot to transport them and their supplies safely and efficiently to and from their village allocation.

I realized also there was more to this simple twenty-minute flight than met the eye. Behind Jerry was a whole network of support people. Radio technicians, flight operators who plot courses and keep track of pilots and planes, aircraft mechanics and more. In every way, each of these people working behind the scenes help to bring the Word of God to the Bauzi people just as surely as the Brileys who are physically

translating the New Testament Scriptures into the
Bauzi language.

After a full morning of shooting photos, Jerry and I
were invited by Joyce Briley to have a light lunch in
their jungle home. It was here, over some casual
conversation, that I learned just how skilled my JAARS
pilot and new friend really was.

Jerry had been a helicopter pilot in Vietnam and had
restarted the JAARS helicopter program in Irian Jaya
that had been closed a year earlier for lack of a pilot.
When I asked him how he was able to fly without
proper navigational charts, he gave me a mischievous
little smile and said, "When I arrived, I found no
accurate charts of this part of the country. And sometimes we worked with less-than-adequate equipment.
We in JAARS have very strict safety operating standards,
but sometimes things happen that you have no control
over. Like the time I was flying with a compass that
wasn't working right."

"What happened?" I asked.

"I had been flying to some of the village locations
where I had never been before. There were no charts to
tell me where I was going or what to expect. To get to my
destination, I would draw a course line and follow a
compass reading. I didn't know at the time the compass
was malfunctioning. It was supposed to be the best and
most accurate compass available, and as one who had
been taught to always follow your instruments, I did
exactly that. But when I turned in the direction the
compass was telling me to take, I would find it physically
and emotionally hard to fly the helicopter in that
direction. A helicopter, of course, doesn't care which
direction you fly it, so when I found myself struggling, I
couldn't understand it. I would turn in the compass

direction, then look up and watch were I was going. Then I would look back at my instruments and to my puzzlement, would be flying in the direction I had turned from. Strangely, when I flew the helicopter in the direction it seemed to want to go—the direction that felt right—I always arrived at the exact location I was looking for, even though I was flying all the wrong headings, sometimes as much as forty to sixty degrees off! I never told anyone about this as it didn't make sense."

Jerry paused for a moment, and shook his head. "You know, I can hardly believe I am telling you this, because if I had heard another pilot telling you this, I would have said the guy is crazy to fly over the jungle like that. The rule is that you always fly by time and heading."

"How did you confirm that your compass was giving you wrong information?" I asked.

"One day I was coming in over our JAARS hangar area flying northwest and I turned southwest. But when I looked at the compass, it was still reading that I was going northwest. At that moment a light dawned in my head and I said, 'Something is wrong here.'

"The next day I had a sling load to take to a village and the compass was pointing sixty degrees off to the right. But I didn't know exactly where I was. To make matters worse, the load hanging below the helicopter began to swing badly. As I considered the problem of the swinging load and the sixty-degree heading, a verse of Scripture came to me: 'My spirit will be behind you directing you, going to the right and to the left, saying this is the way.'

" 'Lord,' I prayed, 'this verse is probably out of context, but I need your Spirit to guide me to the village.' No sooner did I pray, than another verse from James came into my mind: 'You have not because you ask not. And when you ask, you ask for the wrong motives and spend it on your own pleasure.'

" 'Okay, Lord,' I said, 'this isn't for my pleasure. It's for the translators and their families. They need this load to stop swinging. If it doesn't stop in a few moments, I'll have to get rid of it.'

"I slowed down a bit and slowly the load came under control. But now I had the problem of my heading. I again tried to follow the compass and turn to the sixty-degree heading it indicated, but it didn't seem right and I went right back to the previous heading. I decided I would see what happened and asked the Lord to get me to the village. No sooner had I prayed than all of a sudden I looked in front of me and I was flying directly toward the village and the center line of the runway!

"When I landed, the translators greeted me by saying, 'We've been standing here watching you for a long time. You were coming right toward us all the time.' I was dumbfounded, but I guess I shouldn't have been."

"Why not?" I said. "I'm sure I would have been."

"The Lord miraculously saved my life in Vietnam when a door flew off and shattered the tail rudder of my Army helicopter," said Jerry. "I landed in the middle of a mine field on top of a little hill of newly-plowed earth! It's amazing how much one can think about in a short period of time. Believing I was going to die, I thought about my new wife, and I thought about the Lord. About how that in a few moments I was going to meet Somebody that I had professed to know but in reality didn't know very well at all. After I walked away from that near-death experience, I vowed to change all that and get to know the Lord better."

"Did this experience contribute to your decision to become a JAARS pilot?" I asked.

"Yes. I feel God called me to do a job that has eternal results. I can't think of anything more important than giving people the Scriptures in their own language.

"Back to your question about how I'm able to fly with charts that say 'Data Incomplete.' I quickly learned that the Lord didn't wave goodbye to me when I left the States. He's here with me, always, no matter where I am!"

— 11 —

Every Day a Miracle

I believe the essential principle of Bible translation is to communicate the text with the same force as the original hearers experienced the text (with certain allowance for culture, time and distance).

"No one can fully achieve this, but a good translator must strive for this effect. I don't think it can be too fully stressed that the original authors wrote in a form that was natural and idiomatic at the time of their writing."

The man who wrote these words died on August 10, 1980. His name was John Beekman, Wycliffe's first International Translation and Linguistic Coordinator. I wrote about John and his wife Elaine in the book, *Man with the Noisy Heart.*[9] My friend Jim Hefley also wrote about the Beekmans in his book, *Peril by Choice.*[10]

John Donne said it best when he wrote, "... any man's death diminishes me, because I am involved in mankind; and therefore I never send to know for whom the bell tolls; it tolls for thee." (In his world without mass communication, a person's death was announced by the ringing of the church bell.)

I felt about John's death as I felt about the death of C.S. Lewis, and my own dear mother-in-law—as if a great warm light had suddenly gone out and I was left on a dark windswept moor, cold and alone.

John Beekman influenced me more than he realized and more than I realized. The week of his death I was to have met with him to discuss a project that I had worked on for several years (and am still working on). It was a series of lectures I wanted to develop into a book on the nature of creativity, narration, story and related areas of composition.

John, too, had been working on a similar theme he called discourse analysis, or literary semantic analysis. Said John to me one day, "This is the most interesting and exciting linguistic work in which I've been involved. The literary semantic analysis that our translation team did on Acts brought to light a whole new dimension to the Book that I had not realized existed.

"The technique of progressive division and subdivision into sections, paragraphs and propositions put the Book as a whole and its constituent parts into a perspective that I don't think has been or could be achieved in any other way. What I had previously seen as a series of historical accounts, I now see as a literary work of art with balanced structure and obvious design."

It was John Beekman perhaps more than any one single person in Wycliffe who brought into focus the reality that translation is more than a wooden linguistic process in which one replaces the words of one language for the words of another.

Some years ago, one ethnic person received a translation of the Gospel of Mark translated without an awareness of the benefits of discourse analysis. After examining the Gospel, the man said with tragic humor, "Now we have God's Word in two languages we don't understand—Spanish and our own!" The proliferation of translation and linguistic workshops, the training of consultants worldwide and the dissemination of practical Bible translation principles are all designed to counteract a recurrence of this situation.

As of this writing, Wycliffe has assigned translation teams in over 1,000 languages in forty different countries. There have been 233 translated New Testaments with a projected number of completed New Testaments expected at the rate of 20 per year.

The acceleration of accurate intelligible versions of the translated Scriptures is due in large measure to the extraordinary vision and loving practical help John Beekman gave in his role of International Translation Coordinator. Only eternity will reveal the extent and depth of John's influence both to individual translator (in the past and in the years to come) and to the many thousands of ethnic peoples who today and in the future have and will receive an accurate and intelligible translation of the Scriptures in their language. This chapter is written as a tribute both to John Beekman and his courageous and beautiful wife Elaine.

* * * * *

There was never any heart truly great and gracious that was not also tender and compassionate.
                    — Robert South (1634-1716)

Ever since that October day in 1955 when Dr. Charles Hufnagel implanted a plastic valve into John Beekman's deteriorating aortic artery, John became a living miracle. Before that difficult and, by current heart operation technology, primitive operation, Dr. Hufnagel warned John he had only a fifty-fifty chance of survival. "Furthermore," predicted Dr. Hufnagel, "if you do survive, your life expectancy will probably be five years of restricted activity."

Dr. Hufnagel had all the clinical evidence for making such a prediction, but he didn't reckon with John's iron will nor his profound faith and deep personal trust in Jesus Christ. Nor did Dr. Hufnagel reckon with God's plan for John and his delight to use weak vessels to carry out his will. John Beekman lived a full twenty years beyond Dr. Hufnagel's prediction!

And contrary to living a "restricted" life, John filled those twenty-five years to the brim with some of the most important and extraordinary contributions to the cause of Bible translation worldwide. But to list all his translation achievements, or his collaboration of the New Testament for the Chol people of southern Mexico, or his directorship of Wycliffe's Guatemala Branch, or the spark behind the production of translation helps like the commentary compilations and the literary-semantic analysis of the New Testament books, plus his co-authorship of the book *Translating the Word of God,*[11] or the training of a whole cadre of translation consultants, is to see only one side of this unusally dedicated man.

John's secretary, Eleanor McAlpine, gives an important clue into the other side of John's character and why he was so beloved by his family, the Chols, other people, friends and colleagues. "When I worked with John in Mexico, he quietly encouraged me to have my teeth straightened, and I did. He was interested in me as a person and my development in every way."

Dr. Robert Longacre, a close friend and international linguistic consultant in Dallas, gave a further insight into John's "other" side. "John had the ability to reach into a person and turn on a key that opened up a new vision and enabled a person to become greater than himself."

This quality for inspiring transcendence, as I myself found while working with him on the book, *The Man with the Noisy Heart,*[12] is a hallmark of John's character. In so many different ways, John lived out his oft-repeated dictum: "The most effective and lasting way to bring about change is to introduce change in the inner man." John's concept of self-correction, or showing a person how he could overcome or solve a problem himself, was something he sometimes, to his own peril, acted out.

Longtime friend and colleague, Richard Anderson related this interesting anecdote.

"One afternoon at our translation center in Ixmiquil-pan, Mexico, I saw John clamber up to a fifteen-foot wooden platform by a huge mesquite tree. Above the platform, dangling from one of the tree's stoutest branches, was a wrist-thick rope. Swinging off this platform was one of the all-time favorite pastimes of the translators' children. Hardly believing what I was seeing, John deliberately grabbed the rope and with a quick kick, swung free from the platform to make a huge Tarzan-like arc, then landed safely back on the platform. With amazement, I raced over to the platform. When I arrived, John was back on the ground talking with his eight-year-old son. I could hear that valve of his clicking more vigorously than normal.

" 'Why in the world would you do such a thing?' I sputtered. With his characteristic boyish grin that seemed always to hide some mischievous air, John said simply, 'I have a son who is afraid he can't do it. I wanted to show him he can.' "

Said George Cowan, past president of Wycliffe Bible Translators, "I don't think it's *what* John has done that has impacted Wycliffe as much as *how* he did it." And how he did it was with kindness and compassion.

Edna Jane Travis, a longtime friend, colleague and assistant to John on his many projects, including the important, *Translating the Word of God,*[13] summed up this kindness in a letter she once wrote to John:

". . . I wish there was some way I could begin to tell you how marvelous it is for me to have such confidence in you. To know that you can see what the problems are and how best to solve them. And to know that if I even brought you a stupid problem (which I have on occasion) you would never make *me* feel stupid. Thank you for always being so kind and considerate.

"And because of your willingness to listen, you have helped me so much with my personal problems too. You have the ability to see things from all angles and the thoughtfulness and understanding to be able to give not only correct, but sympathetic guidance.

"Another of your qualities I admire tremendously is your courage. Of course, your courage in the face of physical pain and discomfort is obvious. But recently, I have become aware of other kinds of courage. For example, the courage to be yourself. The courage to exercise your freedoms. Freedom to tease (which you always do appropriately), freedom to discuss all kinds of topics, freedom to have new ideas linguistically and to put them into practice, and so on up and down a long list. So, thank you for being your wonderful self."

Examples of John's kindness and compassion as expressed by Edna Jane went hand-in-glove with his sensitivity to the translator who was discouraged and ready to quit. Intuitively, John knew that hard critiquing and criticism, or put-downs in the guise of humor, were terrible blocks to a translator's creativity and individual self-worth. They were, in fact, mistakes against God's intentions for interpersonal relationships.

Richard Anderson remembers what it was like before John had implemented translation and linguistic workshops; before there was a methodology for Bible translation.

"I was ready to quit being a translator and do some other work within Wycliffe," said Richard. "But one day, a week after I had had my translation of Mark torn apart by a translation consultant, I was scheduled to work with John. When the time arrived, we worked through a whole chapter and John said, 'I like what you're doing. It's good. There are a couple of spots where you might like to consider . . .' John then made some helpful suggestions but he always spoke with gentle encouragement. Never once did he deflate or in any way put down what I was doing. With that feeling of support, I eventually went on to complete the New Testament for the Cuicatec people of Mexico."

At this very moment, hundreds of trained translation consultants and Bible translators are carrying on John Beekman's Bible translation principles—and being careful to implement them in the same caring way.

When I learned that John had died, I phoned Elaine to offer my sympathy and express how deeply I cared for her and John. I found myself overcome. In that moment, it was Elaine, after the pattern of her husband, who ministered to me. "Every day he lived was a miracle," said Elaine. And then she briefly told me how early Sunday morning, August 10, John had awakened hemorrhaging from the mouth. "Immediately my son Gary and I rushed him to the hospital," said Elaine.

"Enroute John said, 'I'll be gone before we get there.' Then he reached out and touched me and said, I love you, Mommy. I love you, Gary. I've had a wonderful life . . . a wonderful family . . . God is so good!' Then with a happy laugh, suggesting surprise and joy, he said softly, 'I'm going now!' "

The actual pronouncement of death was at 2:59 a.m. However, that was after nearly forty-five minutes of trying to get his heart going by injections, shock and CPR.

Elaine continued, "We had just celebrated our thirty-fourth wedding anniversary that Friday and the week before was a special time for us all. It seemed John found some special thing with which to compliment and encourage us." Elaine paused for a moment, then said, "And now John has a new body. He is no longer burdened with that old one."

Elaine is right, of course. The Scriptures promise that Jesus will change our weak mortal bodies and make them like his own (Philippians 3:20,21). And this indeed is a miracle and a hope for all whose trust and faith is in Jesus Christ.

Dr. Don Frantz, translator with his wife Patty to the Blackfoot people of Southern Alberta, Canada, once expressed in a letter to John how the Wycliffe family feels toward John's contribution to Bible translation. And the last sentence of that paragraph also expresses how the Wycliffe family, translators, support personnel, short-term helpers and volunteers all feel toward those who serve with distinction with their gifts, prayers and encouragement.

"Keep up your immeasurable contribution to translation (but don't let them push you too hard!). We don't often tell you what we think of you, but let me try with this observation. There have been few men who have played such an enormous role in the furtherance of the Gospel through translation."

I concluded the last chapter of *The Man with the Noisy Heart* with a reaffirmation of John's basic values, his purpose, his vision and his hope for eternity. I can think of no better summation for myself than that which I once wrote for John, namely:

As long as I am here, I want to use whatever strength I have to be of some service in his work. When we think of the greatness and the tenderness of God's love toward us, can we doubt its constancy and final efficacy on our behalf? With Paul the Apostle, I believe that neither death nor anything else in all creation will be able to separate us from the love of God in Jesus Christ our Lord.

— 12 —

Seat 15-H

Welcome aboard, Sir. Your seat is through the galley and to your right." I smiled my thanks to the flight attendant, followed her directions and eased into seat 15-H. I was on a return flight from Dallas, Texas where I had just concluded several interviews for the book that became Wycliffe's fiftieth anniversary volume, *Pass the Word*.[14]

I had reserved my ticket almost a month before the trip and had asked for an aisle seat in the no-smoking section. When no one sat in the seat next to mine, I sighed in relief. I'll have the whole trip to read, I thought. As much as I enjoy people, I sometimes find it difficult to talk to strangers, particularly when I'm tired. I know it's incumbent upon me to always have an answer of the hope that lies within me, but sometimes I'm a reluctant servant. My excuse is that I don't have the gift of gab; that I write better than I speak. But I know, of course, these are lamentable excuses!

On one flight to Calgary as I conversed with my seat companion, I found myself praying for the right words, but they just didn't seem to come. I felt frustrated and totally inept. When we parted, however, he said, "You know, I've spoken to a lot of people who have talked to me about God and Jesus Christ. But you are the first one who has let me do most of the talking. Thank you."

After stowing my battered leather shoulder bag that doubles as my camera bag (I try to keep a low profile with my camera), I pulled out a book and settled back to a quiet, uninterrupted reading time. About five minutes before takeoff, I noticed the plane was almost half empty. When the flight attendants made their last safety check through the cabin, I was still alone. And then, just as the captain ordered the flight attendants to be seated for takeoff, I sensed a presence standing beside me in the aisle.

I looked up and saw an attractive woman in her late twenties or early thirties. She looked at me, smiled, waved her boarding pass and said with a low degree of sexual energy, "Wanna have some company?" I blinked, nodded toward the window seat and said, "Your seat's waiting for you." I stood up to let her pass, then rebuckled and continued to read my book—but not with the same intensity. After takeoff, when the plane had leveled off at its assigned altitude, I began to read in my normal fashion, underlining words with a red felt-tip pen and writing comments in the margins.

It was some time before I again sensed this woman looking at me. "Why are you marking up your book?" she said as I looked up.

Half-embarrassed, I laughed and explained that it helped me remember the author's main points and that I usually made my own index of ideas, facts, statements, truths or insights that appealed to me.

"Are you a teacher?" she asked.

"No, I'm a writer," I said.

"A writer. How interesting. What sorts of things do you write?"

"Mostly books."

"What kind? Would I know any? I like to read."

And so began another in-flight conversation. I closed my book and we exchanged business cards. I learned her name was Susan and that she was an art dealer with her own shop in Indianapolis. She was clearly a woman of the eighties—liberated and self-assured. Her inquisitive probing mind seldom yielded to my analysis or conclusions without asking leading questions about how or why I'd reached them.

As we passed through the time zones, I spoke about God and the need for transcendence in one's life to give it ultimate meaning. Susan said that art gave her meaning, but admitted she often looked for more out of life than what she was presently experiencing.

"This faith in Christ you talk about, is it objective or subjective?" she asked.

"What a great question!" I said. "Greater minds than mine have written tomes on this interesting and perplexing question."

"I would like to hear your opinion."

"I think knowing Jesus Christ as one's personal Friend and Savior involves both," I said.

"How can that be?" There was a slight edge of condescension in her voice, as if she had found a chink in my armor.

"It's because a true believer's faith in Jesus Christ involves two kinds of knowing. One kind is knowing concrete historical facts about God and why Jesus came to earth in the first place. In a sense, we can only believe what we know or intelligently apprehend. The Bible tells us that Jesus Christ died on a Roman cross to pay the price of our individual sin."

"I don't know about all this sin bit," said Susan.

"Basically," I explained, "sin is living one's life independently from God."

"Okay, but let's get back to the question of faith being objective or subjective."

"The Bible tells me a great deal about who Jesus is and why He came to earth and how much He loved people. I can therefore objectively say, I know about God, about his plan for the redemption of mankind and about his promise to give eternal life to all who will accept and believe these truths. That's informational.

"But when a true believer in Christ says, 'I know God; I know Jesus loves me and I have invited Him into my life' he or she has gone beyond a clinical observation. Let me make an analogy.

"In marriage, the kind of marriage I'm acquainted with, merely believing or knowing about a certain girl, does not make me married. Nor does having an intense emotional feeling about her make me married. Only when I made a commitment of my will and said, 'I do,' did I receive my wife into my life and establish a relationship with her. The Bible says becoming a true Christian is a lot like getting married. It involves this same kind of commitment—commitment of intellect, emotion and will. It means I enter into a dynamic relationship with a Living Person, the Lord Jesus Christ.

"I once read a statement that said, 'Reason is ultimately the servant of feeling.' And the French philosopher Pascal told us what this means when he said, 'The heart has its reasons which reason does not know.' This helps me understand the relationship between objectivity and subjectivity. The crucial questions and actions of men and women are ultimately made in the heart. When Christians talk about their born-again experience, they are really talking about a change of outlook—a change of basic attitudes brought about from a heart relationship with God as He meets them through the Person of Jesus Christ."

I don't know if I answered Susan's questions adequately. I do know she was silent for a while. When we were served lunch I asked if I might pray. I think she misunderstood my intention, because she reacted sharply by saying, "I'm not quite ready to make such a decision, and when and if I do, it will be in my own time and in my own way."

When the plane landed in Los Angeles, Susan introduced me to her waiting boyfriend. He was a tall, well-dressed man with a full head of blond hair set on a handsome, deeply-tanned face that flashed a perfect set of teeth. We spoke for a few minutes while we waited for our luggage, but after retrieving her one small suitcase from the carousel, Susan and her boyfriend were off, arm in arm, locked into their own private world.

A few weeks later, I sent Susan *Mere Christianity*[15] by C.S. Lewis along with a letter that said in part:

> In the last book of the New Testament, Revelation 3:20, our lives are compared to a house when Jesus says, "Here I am! I stand at the door and knock. If anyone hears my voice and opens the door, I will come in and eat with him, and he with me." Susan, just as you willingly open the door to your room when a friend knocks, so open the door of your life and invite in the living, loving Person of Jesus Christ. He will never come in without an invitation.
>
> One way to do this is to say a short prayer in your own words—something like, "Jesus, I acknowledge my need of You. I believe in You and in your work of salvation on my behalf. Help me to trust You as

I commit my life to You as Lord and Savior. Amen."

The promise of John 1:12 is, "To all who receive Jesus (who are open and who listen to Him and who trust Him), to those who yield their allegiance to Him, to them He gives the right to become the children of God."

Susan, my prayer for you is that you will indeed invite Jesus Christ into your life (as you said, in your own time and in your own way). I pray you won't wait too long.

My prayer for Susan is the same prayer Norma and I have for each and every one who has not yet invited Jesus Christ into his or her life. We pray you won't wait too long.

— 13 —

I'm Losing my Job
and I'm Happy

In 1956 Norma and I, under God's leading, first committed ourselves to work with Wycliffe Bible Translators. At the time, we had no idea how all this might affect our two preschool children. As it turned out, the Lord blessed us with two more children on our first assignment in Mexico. Currently, three are married and have established homes of their own and, if asked about their cross-cultural experiences, they will tell you they have only fond and happy memories. (Our fourth child, Karen, was only five months old when we left Mexico for Chicago to assume responsibilities as Wycliffe's Regional Director for the eight north-central states.)

I said all three married children have established homes of their own. That is not entirely correct. Our third child, Lee, has responded with his wife, Paula, to the same call that captivated Norma and me in 1956: namely, to commit themselves to serving God through Bible translation. As of this writing, Lee and Paula have been accepted as Members-in-Training with Wycliffe and are completing their SIL training in Dallas, Texas.

Let me hasten to add a parenthesis. In no way do I consider a career in Wycliffe as the only way to serve

God. On the contrary, one can express his or her service to God in whatever walk of life one feels the leading of the Spirit of God.

I say all this to relate that, while Lee was studying at Wheaton College, he was quietly asking God to give him direction for his life's work. And while he was leaning toward a career with Wycliffe, he wasn't entirely certain that Bible translation was what he ought to do. To gain some practical experience, he took time out after his junior year at Wheaton and spent seven months in Papua New Guinea under a Wheaton-sponsored program to Third World countries called "Human Needs and Global Resources" (HNGR).

Halfway through his project of building a wooden waterwheel to generate electricity, Lee accepted the invitation of Wycliffe translators' Neil and Carol Anderson to visit them in their village allocation.

After a hard seven-hour hike over extremely slippery and steep, muddy, leech-infested trails that required an unexpected overnight under a hunter's flimsy lean-to, Lee arrived at the Anderson house. (They now use the facilities of a JAARS helicopter.)

For the next two weeks, Lee lived, observed and interacted with the Andersons as they interacted with the Podopa people.

Often it's difficult to pinpoint exactly the moment or under what specific circumstance God has broken through with a new insight or direction for one's life. And so it was with Lee, except that after his two weeks with the Andersons, he somehow knew that God wanted him to become a Bible translator.

The following story is related in appreciation to the Andersons for their positive ministry in a young man's life at a crucial time in his history. But more importantly, this story illustrates what God is about in his world and the part Bible translation is playing in the whole scheme of HIS STORY.

For an hour, the Podopa villagers knew they were coming. Every man and boy who could draw a bow or hurl a spear was alerted. There were only nineteen of them—seventeen with brown skins and two with white—but in the highlands of Papua New Guinea, a group as small as nineteen, if they were warriors, could be a serious threat, even to a village of two or three hundred people.

Large-scale intertribal warfare and cannibalism have been brought under control by government patrols and laws in this independent commonwealth nation. Still, mutual hostility, hatred, distrust and generations of intertribal skirmishes die hard. Particularly is this true in the highlands, where harsh rugged mountains and deep valleys of swamps and marshes are formidable barriers for government agencies to break through and exercise their authority. Coupled with this is the barrier of language and custom. Tucked away in the highland mountains, along tributaries of great rivers and on the hot coastal lands of Papua New Guinea are over 700 ethnic minority peoples, each with their own distinct language and tribal customs. These groups are distinguished by more than geographical isolation; their distinction is also that few of their languages have ever been written down.

And this was the reason for nineteen men being on that slippery leech-infested trail that day. The two white skins were members of Wycliffe Bible Translators and its sister organization, the Summer Institute of Linguistics. The leader of the group was Neil Anderson, a John

Denver look-alike who, with his pretty wife Carol, has worked with the Podopa people since 1973, reducing their language to writing, giving them an alphabet, teaching them to read and write, and translating portions of the Old and New Testament. And now Neil, a Wycliffe colleague and seventeen Podopa believers were on a missionary journey.

The villagers had heard the news on the "jungle telegraph." Men with hands cupped to their mouths had yelled the announcement from hamlet to hamlet: "Nineteen unknown men on the trail. Tell everyone they are coming your way." The villagers were ready when the group of men entered the village. Standing in a ragged semi-circle were the older men, leaders of the village. These in turn were flanked by younger men clasping their five-foot hunting bows and arrows. Most of the men were adorned with shell necklaces. The women stood behind the men and most wore beaten bark capes that fell from their heads and covered only their backs. Many held babies on their hips.

Young children had run away when Neil and the other men first entered the village. Now they trickled back and, between the strong muscular legs of their fathers, they shyly peered at the strangers who had walked unafraid into their village.

Noted for their ability as orators, the men of this highland village were now yelling and speaking in agitated voices. They were nervous and unsure and the yelling helped to relieve some of the electric tension. Everyone wanted to know who they were, where they had come from and why they had come to see them.

No one immediately volunteered to answer their questions. It was proper Podopa etiquette to remain silent. No Podopa man wanted to appear boastful or assume a position of authority without the approval of his peers. Also, the visiting Podopa men were not altogether sure who the leaders were in this village. Protocol demanded they address only the men in authority.

There was also another item of polite courtesy that had to be observed before they stated their business. They had to finish chewing their eighteen-inch sticks of raw sugar cane that the villagers passed around. This common highland courtesy was much like offering a visitor in a Western home a cup of coffee, glass of juice or soft drink.

At last, when the visitors had chewed their sugar cane, a young Podopa man began to speak. His name was Hweade (Thomas). He had a high, clear forehead, thick, curly black hair and an infectious smile.

"You people wonder why we have come," said Thomas. "You wonder why we are traveling around these mountains when there are enemies who might want to kill us. I will tell you why. We are here to tell you about what we have been doing in our village. We are excited to tell you that we have been working on the New Testament—putting the Words of God and of his Son Jesus Christ into a Book. More than twelve of us have been the ones to write this down. We have also been learning to read and write. And we ourselves have made books about our stories and legends.

"We also have in our village a water system. We can now wash off the thick mud from our bodies and we no longer have to carry water in bamboo tubes. The water comes all by itself to a wash house. We have a sawmill and we can make doors and windows for our houses. All this we have done. And we want to tell you how you can also have such things. Tonight we want to have a meeting here to read from this new Book called Acts. We want to tell you something about what God is like. This is the true God, the One Who made everything we see and eat. If you come tonight, we will read and sing and tell you more about what we are doing in our village."

* * * * *

From the beginning of their ministry as Bible translators among the 2,500 Podopa people, Neil and Carol wanted to work themselves out of a job. They, with their four children, have lived in the Podopa village of Pukuta (about 350 people) as good neighbors. Neil has stitched and bandaged wounds, pulled teeth, built a village water system by laying two miles of pipe from a spring above the village and has performed many other practical helps.

And Carol, in between teaching her children, has typed language materials and worked on the art and layout of reading primers and storybooks. It has been the kind of work and ministry that Neil and Carol could happily do for many years—perhaps all their career lives. Yet, Neil knew that if the 120 baptized Podopa believers were to grow strong spiritually, they had to assume an active responsibility for the translation of the New Testament and the evangelization of the Podopa people.

Neil has not preached or functioned in the way usually associated with what a missionary is "supposed" to do. Rather, he has worked as one among equals with twelve or more men over the translation desk, talking and explaining the meaning of Scripture. These Podopa men have functioned as co-translators, working with Neil as they translate.

It has been out of this intimate, day-by-day association

that the Podopa co-translators have caught the vision to become missionaries to their own people.

Several years before Neil and Carol were assigned to work with the Podopas, an itinerant evangelist from another tribal group walked those treacherous trails to preach to the people in the village of Pukuta. After his preaching service, he said,"I must move on to other villages. But I want you to pray that God will send someone to teach you more about what it means to have faith in Jesus Christ." When Neil and Carol asked for permission to live in the village of Pukuta, the believers and others said, "Yes, of course. You are the ones we have been praying for!"

Just as that itinerant evangelist had called the people to pray, so Neil and Carol later challenged the Podopa believers to pray for the other seventeen Podopa villages. Neil would remind them that he had not only come to serve the people of one village. There were others that needed the gospel, too. But such a notion at first was beyond the imagination of the Podopa believers. There were no roads—only slippery, muddy trails infested with horrible leeches. It would take weeks to trek to all seventeen villages and besides, it meant going through hostile territory. "It can't be done," they would say. But Neil and Carol believed and prayed.

The group of Podopa co-translators continued their translation work and, as they worked on Acts and read about Paul's missionary journeys, they began to be increasingly motivated to reach out to other villages. Some of the men said, "The same things that have happened in Acts should happen in our area. There is a village twelve hours away from us. They don't know anything about the Lord. Let's go down there and read to them these new words from Acts."

It took Neil and his companions four long, hard weeks of trekking through the Eastern highlands of Papua New Guinea, but they did indeed reach all seventeen villages. And in every village, it was the Podopa believers from Pukuta who did the talking. While one man told why they had come, another would talk about how they were learning to read and write and explain how they made their own books of stories and legends. Still another would explain how their water system worked.

And in the special evening meetings, with one or two kerosene lamps to dispel the thick darkness, the Podopa believers would sing special songs and then read from the Book of Acts. When they finished reading, they would ask, "How does that sound?" The response was usually, "That sounds good." And the Podopa men from Pukuta would say, "We're glad you like it because now we want to tell you the meaning of these words. The old ways of our people were the ways of killing, but these words tell us something new. It's the way of love. It's the way of Jesus Christ."

And while the Podopa men would explain the gospel, Neil Anderson would squat at the edge of the circle of orange light and smile to himself. In each village, as the Podopa believers themselves explained the Good News of Jesus Christ, he knew he was losing his job, but he was happy.

— 14 —

One Down and Five to Go

One of the most striking characteristics of the creative person is his openness to the events and feelings that touch his or her life. I have tried (I don't always succeed) to be consciously aware of what is happening around me. Particularly is this true when I am on an assignment. I want to note carefully the colors, sounds, smells and sights and scrutinize an individual's characteristics—their clothes and how they're worn, their height, hair, skin, smile, teeth and the way he or she walks, gestures and much more. Details allow me to bring a character or place to life and give the reader an experience of another world or people. These are some of the tools of the trade that help a writer become a better craftsman. But there is another dimension to writing that is infinitely more important. Namely, being open to the Holy Spirit's guidance in the simple, mundane affairs of one's daily life.

I arrived in Guatemala City in the first week of November 1985 (I had already been in Mexico City and just missed the great earthquake by hours) to discover the city was in the grips of a severe gas shortage. Martha King, translator of the Central Cakchiquel New Testa-

ment had volunteered to drive me to several outlying
areas where Cakchiquel teams were working together
on translation. The only problem was gas. Martha had
enough for part of the proposed trip but needed to keep
some in reserve for an important trip several days later.
She also wasn't entirely sure that all the teams I wanted
to see and photograph would be in their locations. And
there was no possible way for us to contact them ahead
of time.

"I've been in many situations like this before," I said
to Martha and Bob Whitesides, Director of SIL's work
in Guatemala. "Since it's not my car, I know it's easy for
me to say let's go and trust God to guide us to a gas
station that will sell us gas and that I'm sure I'll be able
to see all the people I've planned to see. But I have a
hundred different stories of how God opened up the
way when things seemed completely impossible. It's a
step of risky faith."

My time in Guatemala was limited so when a colleague
promised Martha a couple of extra gallons of gas, we
left on our proposed trip. On the outskirts of the city we
came to a gas station that, to our surprise, had none of
the customary half-mile car lineups. We drove in and
asked innocently if they had gas for sale. Even though it
wasn't our authorized day to purchase gas, the attendant
let us buy three gallons. An hour down the highway we
came to two naked gas pumps along the side of the
road. There were a couple of trucks in line and we fell in
behind them. When our turn came, the attendant filled
the gas tank without asking any questions. Martha
thought this was indeed a quiet miracle. And for the
remainder of that long, fact-finding day, we experienced
one quiet miracle after another. All of the teams were in
place. "Quite by accident," we ran into Mauro Canú,

the director of the Cakchiquel Multiple Translation Project. I had wanted to photograph him but Martha had no idea where we might find him. Martha was sure we would miss one team's devotional time, but we arrived just as they were beginning. And in the town of San Antonio we "accidentally" met a woman who had personally known Uncle Cam and his first wife Elvira when they came to live in San Antonio in 1920. And there were more examples of what could only be described as God's leading for that occasion.

I don't mean to suggest that nothing goes wrong on my fact-finding trips. I have had my share of delays and breakdowns and unexpected and prolonged waits in airports. Nor do I want to ascribe a magical formula to God's guidance. But what I have noticed is that when I am completely thrown on the Lord without any resources at my disposal, He is faithful and does as Psalm 32:8 says:

I will instruct you and teach you in the way you should go; I will counsel you and watch over you.

Here, then, is the story that came out of my fact-finding trip to discover what God is doing through the Cakchiquel Multiple Translation Project.

When Martha King and her partner Jo Ann Munson began working among the 100,000 Central Cakchiquel people of Guatemala in 1967, they appeared to have an almost ideal translation situation. There were none of the often painful and frustrating obstacles of indifference or resentment from the local people. There were a number of churches already established and there were lay leaders and pastors who had assumed the responsibility for evangelism and preaching among their own people. The pressing need, as determined by SIL survey teams, was for an up-to-date idiomatic translation of the New Testament and the implementation of an ongoing literacy program.

Almost at once, the Lord led Martha and Jo Ann to two well-educated Cakchiquel people. One was Mauro Canú who, while checking Martha's translated materials, also began to do initial drafts of many New Testament books, and he soon became Martha's co-translator.

The other was Debora Ruyan who, with her editorial and typing skills, became Jo Ann's colleague in literacy. Heavily involved in weekly Bible classes in her church, she was an ideal person to help develop a literacy program that would prepare readers for the New Testament when it was published. (Debora was later joined by her two sisters, Dorcas and Lucia, who proofread manuscripts and typed stencils.)

For the next several years, Martha and her teammates worked with diligence and enthusiasm. But then several realities began to emerge. One was the deeply pervasive notion among the Cakchiquel believers that their language was not worthy of being used to express spiritual truths. It had been one of Martha's sub-goals in her translation program to create an awareness and appreciation for the use of the Cakchiquel language in church services, but since Spanish was considered the prestige language and the language of upward mobility and commerce, many Cakchiquel pastors often preached in Spanish.

But there was more than economics involved in the Cakchiquel's seeming preference for Spanish over their own language. In the minds of many was the notion that being able to read Spanish was part of their religion—a kind of sacrament. It didn't matter if you couldn't understand the words you said. The important thing was to be able to pronounce the Spanish words.

Apart from the practical considerations of not fully understanding what was being said in Spanish was the damage being done to the Cakchiquel's self esteem. It is a fundamental fact that how one feels about his language and culture is related to how one feels about himself. Martha learned that the Cakchiquels generally felt poorly about themselves. It was as if they were experiencing a kind of cultural asphyxiation by the larger Spanish-speaking community—mostly because their language was only spoken and they didn't have any books or printed materials.

The second problem had to do with the translation itself. It had been Martha's vision that she and Mauro Canú could produce a translation that would serve the entire Cakchiquel area that encompassed over 150,000 speakers. But after they had translated the Gospel of Mark and a number of Old Testament stories, they discovered the Central Cakchiquel translation would not adequately serve the other five Cakchiquel areas (the Solola, North Central, South Central, South and South Western) without substantive dialectical changes. This presented the need of separate New Testaments for each of the six Cakchiquel areas. Additionally, there were at least nine sub-dialects of the Central Cakchiquel language that would require special changes and adaptations.

When the Central Cakchiquel New Testament was dedicated on September 27, 1981, many of Martha's friends wondered if her work was now over. She lost no time in explaining that in reality her work was just beginning. She had at least five more translations to go!

To meet the challenge, Martha and Mauro began praying and looking for Cakchiquel men whom they could train to take over the exacting task of making the adaptations to their own dialect areas, using the Central translation as their guide. "My new job," wrote Martha, "will consist of training, overseeing and checking the work of what is now being called the Cakchiquel Multiple Translation Project (CMTP)." (Assisting in the Southwestern Cakchiquel area were Terry and Gaylyn Whalin from Whittier, California.)

Earlier, the thought of being involved in at least five more translation projects almost overwhelmed Martha. But one day the Lord spoke to her through two verses of Scripture. The first was Ephesians 3:20 (NIV):

Now to him who is able to do immeasurably more than all we ask or imagine, according to his power that is at work within us . . .

The second was sent to Martha by a friend:

We are praying, too, that you will be filled with his mighty glorious strength, so that you can keep going no matter what happens—always full of the joy of the Lord   (Colossians 1:11 Living Bible).

Many times over the years, Martha has gained inspiration and vision from the truth of these verses. During the first year of recruitment, not a single person expressed a willingness to work on translation. But Martha and Mauro kept praying and by the second year, the Lord confirmed their faith by supplying six workers for four areas and five for the remaining areas. The CMTP program was at last under way!

By January 1982, Martha gave a total of twenty-nine Cakchiquel workers an intensive four-week training course in such subjects as Bible translation principles, reading and writing Cakchiquel, Cakchiquel grammar, Bible history, geography, Mayan culture and other things. Included in the "other things," was a special emphasis on the reality that God made all languages and none was superior to any other.

Admittedly, it was a small beginning on the road to helping the Cakchiquel believers gain a greater sense of self-worth and appreciation for their language and culture—but it was a beginning. "I wanted them to fully understand that it was God Who had given them their language," said Martha, "and I wanted them to be captivated by the richness of their own beautiful language."

As the CMTP program gained momentum, so did the need for funds. In a letter home she wrote, "I had been asking God to supply the funds in order that I would not have to go into debt to pay Mauro or suspend the program. As I lay in bed one night with this burden heavy on my heart, I asked specifically that God would supply the following day. And He did! God gave me the needed confirmation to continue through some of his children whom I had never met."

The "God's children" Martha wrote about were the many Wycliffe Associates who, through their special insight and vision, pledged and gave of their funds to keep this important Bible translation program alive.

There is, of course, much yet to be done. But much has already been accomplished. In the Southwest Cakchiquel area, the believers invited Martha to a dedication service for the first two books (Mark and James) produced by the translation team. When Martha pulled up in front of the church after a long, hot, dusty ride from Guatemala City, the first thing she saw was a big banner spread across the street. On it were the words, "THE WORD OF GOD IS NOW IN OUR LANGUAGE."

In yet another area where the concept of using Cakchiquel had been particularly low, Martha reported on the reaction of the men working on the CMTP committee. "As we began to check the Gospel of John, I was excited to hear the chuckles and other reactions by the men as they followed along while it was being read. I could tell the words were coming alive for them. And there were tears. Tears as the realization broke over them that God had indeed made their language. It could be written. It had worth."

Faith Without Works is Dead

For him, it was like Walden's Pond—a temporary escape from the demands of village life and the intensity of the translation desk. The geography was different of course. Thoreau's pond was on the outskirts of Concord, Massachesetts; my translator friend lived in an Ecuadorian rain forest.

Like Thoreau, my friend was something of a naturalist, and he found himself at ease amid the flora and fauna of the *Oriente* (the eastern province of Ecuador's vast Upper Amazon Basin). He enjoyed this special relationship not only with the natural elements of the forest, but also with the cultivated crops and cattle he raised on his small experimental farm. His purpose was to encourage the ethnic peoples he worked with to upgrade their own farming methods and improve their livestock.

There was a certain flinty independence and self-reliance about my friend. I don't suppose he was quite the social critic Thoreau was, but he did have an uncluttered practical view of how people who call themselves Christians ought to live. And one afternoon he invited me to go to his pond to fish and talk.

The pond was an easy half-hour's walk through a thick phalanx of trees—great mahoganies and silk-cottons that have their own flying buttresses to support their great bulk. The trees, mostly branchless to their crowns—perhaps two hundred feet above the jungle floor—all fight a desperate battle for survival as they strive to outreach one another through the gloomy canopy to the life-giving light above.

The earth squished beneath my shoes as I made my way over the narrow, winding trail. It was like hundreds I had been over before—wet and damp and covered with leaves. At one point, my friend stopped and pushed over a tree the size of a telephone pole as easily as if it had been standing free without roots. "Termites," he said. "On the outside the tree looks as sound as any other, but its core has been eaten. Remember what Jesus said about the Pharisees? They looked beautiful on the outside, but inside they were filled with dead bones."

At last we arrived at his pond. It wasn't a pretty pond as ponds go. The water was brown and cluttered with twigs, branches and fallen logs that looked like the bleached bones of a long-departed dinosaur.

"Just splash the tip of your rod in the water," said my friend, "then cast in your line."

What a strange way to fish, I thought. No self-respecting trout or salmon fisherman would do it this way. Nevertheless I did as instructed and sure enough, no sooner had I slapped the water and cast in my line when a fish took my hook. It was small, ugly-looking and about the size of a tom cod or small brook trout. Surprisingly, I got another and another. My friend wasn't getting any action—and he wasn't pleased! And then I snagged my line on a log. "Just leave it," he said.

"I'll get it another day." I was disappointed. This was beginning to be fun! But I hadn't come to Ecuador to fish; I had work to do. And I began my interview.

One of my standard interview questions has to do with the person's own spiritual development and growth. I am sincerely interested in discovering the ways God brings about character development and insight, how a person's thinking may have changed over the years and how a person has come to terms with his own limitations, vulnerabilities and unrealized dreams. Usually, people are willing to share and reflect on what God is teaching them. I remember, however, how one person sat in stony silence when asked such a question. He looked at me as if I had committed the unpardonable sin!

But there was no such hesitation with my friend. "For many years, I went through the forms of Christianity," he said. "I said 'amen' in all the right places and I knew how to *say* prayers, which is different than praying. Christian people need a new vision about prayer, about world mission, about living their daily lives in a truly Christian way."

"I identify with what you're saying," I said. "Explain a little more fully about what you mean by a new vision."

"I mean that without a vision, an enthusiasm, a zeal born out of a grateful heart for what God has done in giving his Son in love for the salvation of all people, we will perish. I mean that we Christians ought to be growing in our faith and devotion and love for our Lord. I mean that we should be learning how to reach out to people in need. When we see people who are hurting, we should be the ones to care and give comfort. And when there are hungry people, we should be the ones to feed them.

"I've struggled with a Christianity that says to be a Christian you pay your bills, don't get drunk or utter profanity. I still believe these are good things, but true Christianity is more. A person without any faith in God could be characterized by these things. I'm interested in the distinctives of a true Christian faith and one of these has to do with the way we love God and other people.

"I believe one of the central reasons why the church has grown strong in our area is because we have given them the Word of God in their own language. This means they can now on their own, at their own speed, in their own cultural way reflect on its message and reason among themselves as to how they will live out its implications.

"But I believe there are other reasons for the church's strength. It has to do with the personal interest we have taken with the people. My wife has cared for their medical needs and I hopefully have shown my care by sharing my life and talking with them about their own hopes, needs and family problems. When we have had concerns about the conduct of our own children, we have shared these with the people and allowed them to minister to us. Furthermore, the people know we will go out of our way to help them. We don't have to go out in the hot sun to work in their fields, but we do. They have also seen the difference between the way we treat them and the pompous attitudes of absentee landlords and hunters of rubber who have treated them like animals without respect or regard for their personhood.

"I think this new vision means to live out my Christian life in both word and deed—to demonstrate in concrete action what I preach."

We left the pond and walked back to his house—a two-story unpainted wooden plank structure set up on stilts with a galvanized tin roof. He had cleared the jungle around the house and only two or three tall mahogany trees stood in the immediate vicinity. There is virtually no twilight in the tropics and we arrived just as darkness came upon us. The soft, orange glow from a kerosene lantern set in the kitchen window welcomed us.

My friend continued to expound on a variety of topics, but central to his theme was his firm conviction that the barometer of a person's commitment to Christ was how he treated others. Faith needed to be lived out in practical reality rather than theory. "Too many Christians let church attendance, tithing and correct theology become a substitute for a hands-on practical ministry among people." he said.

I wondered if my friend's words were too strong or hard or too general a commentary on the church at large. Were they coming from a tender man of steel like the prophet Jeremiah or from one of God's servants like James who said, "Be ye doers of the word, and not hearers only" (James 1:22 KJV)?

When I returned from my trip to South America, I wrote the above observations in my journal and left them there without further comment. I did use my friend's challenge to go beyond a peripheral involvement with people in a Christmas meditation I later gave, but that was that.

I didn't have in my repertoire of experiences a particular story that fully illustrated my friend's strong position until I was about to write the last chapter of this book. That's when I met Paul Townsend (no relation to William Cameron Townsend).

I had gone to Guatemala to gather information for a second volume on the early ministry of William Cameron

Townsend (companion to the first volume, *A Thousand Trails*).[16] One night after a severe tropical downpour, Paul came to the apartment where I was staying for an interview.

The first thing I noticed about Paul was his beard— full, tangled and red! His eyebrows matched his beard as did his thick hair that came low over his brow. But it was his eyes that arrested me. Intense and unsmiling, they seemed to reflect the pain and suffering he had vicariously experienced on behalf of the Ixil people with whom he works.

As Paul unfolded his story, I learned that in the late seventies and early eighties, particularly the years 1979-1982, the dark cloud of agony and terror that hovered over Central America for decades became a deluge of violence and savagery in Guatemala (as well as in El Salvador and Nicaragua). Said one Guatemalan pastor, "We are trapped between the right-and left-wing groups struggling for control. The leftist guerrillas come out of the hills and want food and information. Sometimes they want to use our church building for their own purposes. If we refuse, they accuse us of supporting the right. And when the rightist troops come, they accuse us of cooperating with the left. And thus we are caught in a vicious trap. We are harassed from both sides and what is worse, our people—many, many of our people—have been killed."

One of the ethnic groups caught in the midst of these violent extremes are the 4,500 Ixil people. Like most of Guatemala's ethnic groups, the Ixil are famous for their colorful costumes. The women wear striking loose-fitting over-blouses patterned with geometric designs of greens, blues and reds against a white background, all hand-woven on pre-Columbian back-strap looms. Not to be outdone, the men wear bright red jackets with fancy designs on the back, complimented by a thickly woven belt, also with geometric designs and festooned with tiny tassels. Interestingly, the men's jackets are fashioned after the jackets once worn by Spanish officers during the time of the viceroys.

During the most violent period of the war, from September 1979 to mid-1982, Paul and his wife Sharon and family lived and worked in Guatemala City. A number of Ixils, who had fled the violence of their homeland, found refuge in the city and willingly worked with Paul on the translation of his literacy materials.

Paul's principal task was to encourage the Ixils to become literate in their own language. A growing church had emerged from Scripture translation done by longtime SIL workers, Ray and Helen Elliott. Said Paul, "I was anxious for the Scriptures to be used by the growing churches and wanted to make reading a permanent value among the Ixil. There is no other way for a people to mature spiritually without the practice of routine Scripture reading."

But in September 1982, when Paul returned to begin implementing the reading classes, he found terrible devastation. The daily order and living pattern bore little resemblance to the way things were prior to 1979. The most noticeable was the lack of men. About one quarter of all males had been killed in the conflict. Hundreds of others were living behind guerrilla lines. Many men who had been forced to join the guerrilla movement were now slow to believe the reports that the president had granted an amnesty for all who would give up their arms for hoes.

In the meantime, the responsibility for farming and maintaining the family fell to the wives and widows, most of whom had no housing. Little by little, however, the word seeped into the hills that the then-president, General Efrain Rijos Montt, was as good as his word, and the men began to trickle back.

When Paul and Sharon once again began living among the Ixils, they discovered that food was one of the main reasons for the men's willingness to return. They were starving to death in the hills. "The men who were coming in from the hills," said Paul, "were digging for grubs, shooting little birds—anything to fill their stomachs. When I saw this, I knew I had to do something positive and practical. After all, James says that faith without works is dead."

Working in concert with a large church in Guatemala City—the same church that then-president Rijos Montt attended—Paul and others formed a foundation called, "Aid to Hungry People." This was followed by the church donating a sawmill. "We sawed boards day and night," said Paul, "and then with groups of volunteer men who had come down from the States and elsewhere, we began to build houses for the poorest of the poor widows." [Each house cost about $250.00 U.S. dollars.]

"This," continued Paul, "was a great surprise to the community. The pervading custom is to only do a favor for someone who can return it. If you can help the mayor of the rich landowner or someone with influence, so much the better. It is simply not good business to help someone who is poor, particularly orphans and widows. In Ixil culture, a widow is considered only good enough to be a second wife, yet the church reached out to them, helping them establish their own homes and providing men from the church to help plant their cornfields."

To the further surprise of the community, the church and foundation helped everyone—not just believers. "The war hit everyone." said Paul. "We needed to show our love was like the love of Jesus who welcomed everyone without regard to rank or sex, power or influence."

As the Ixil believers helped their neighbors fix tiles on their roofs, build houses and furniture, prepare fields and plant corn and generally work together in a variety of different ways, their neighbors began to say things like, "I can't believe this is happening, not after all the bloodshed we have experienced. This is wonderful! *This must be the true religion!* I want to understand more of what it means to become an evangelical."

As a result, in the course of a year and a half, in one community, the church grew from one hundred to over six hundred. "All because the people saw we were willing to back up our words with positive acts of love," said Paul.

Not everyone, including some of his own SIL colleagues, applauded Paul and his group for becoming directly involved in the ministry of food distribution. They felt he was being sidetracked from his original goal of helping the Ixils to become literate. But Paul unabashedly declares he could do no less. "The situation demanded that I do something positive. How could I be indifferent to such need? Besides, who wants to learn to read when he's starving?"

However, what Paul's critics and Paul himself never dreamed would happen, happened—the beginning of a strong and ongoing literacy program. "With one hand we would give out milk, beans and corn, and with the other we would teach a literacy class." Those who came to assist Paul in the literacy program also found themselves mixing food distribution and various other relief work with Bible instruction classes.

Paul's story of how, in just three years, he and his literacy team were able to drop the illiteracy rate among the Ixils from 90 to 85 to 80% and of the goal to cut this five to seven percent per year, is worthy of another anthology. But there's another aside to this story. Just before I concluded my interview with Paul that night in Guatemala City, I asked him to tell me what the Ixils think about prayer.

"That's an easy question to answer," said Paul. "The Ixil believers pray more than any people I have ever been associated with, including my own American culture. In fact, one of the things the Ixils have taught me is that I am not a man of real prayer. I pray and I believe prayer is important, but I don't spend hours in prayer like the Ixil do.

"Each week the church conducts an all-night prayer vigil and most of the members attend. Once a month the children from ages six to about ten or eleven have their own all-night prayer vigil."

When I asked what the children did all night, Paul said they had a wonderful time. Besides praying, they sing, play Bible games, listen to Bible stories and read Scriptures.

I was impressed with what Paul was telling me and even more impressed when I asked him to tell me specifically how the Ixils prayed. "The Ixils' prayers," said Paul, "are mostly adoration. It's almost like listening to the Psalms." And then he gave me an example:

Our heavenly Father, God in glory, we thank You
and praise You for this day and this hour; for our

food, for our health, for our mothers and fathers. For our children and our grandchildren. We praise You for our home and our habitation. You are our God. Lord, You are our hope! We trust in You. We depend upon You. We are in your hands. We are at your feet.

"The believers pray this way hour after hour," said Paul. "They adored God even in the midst of their trials when many were without homes or money and didn't know where they were going to get their next meal."

When I asked Paul why he thought the Ixils were able to maintain such confidence in the Lord, he said, "Perhaps it is because they see life and death differently than we in the West. They approach death a little like C.S. Lewis does in the Narnian Chronicles—where one simply passes through the wardrobe and into another sphere where eternal existence with God begins. The Ixils view their earthly part of life as a preparation for the fuller, more complete life to come. In the meantime they pray and take the Scriptures seriously, particularly those Scriptures that admonish them to trust the Lord. They say, 'God knows the best way for our lives.' "

"What a remarkable statement of faith," I said, "It sounds amazingly like the Chamula believers in Mexico who, in the midst of the persecution, said, 'We follow the true road, the right road, the straight road because it is He Who guides us and gives us life.' "

It was late and Paul had been talking non-stop for almost two hours, but I had yet to ask him my standard question. "Paul, in what way has your personal faith and view of life and God changed through these difficult years?"

His answer was forthright and spoken without false piety or superiority. "I'm not the same fun-loving person I once was. I'm more serious and want to give myself more vigorously to the work, even if it requires physical hardship and sacrifice. I feel a deeper sense of urgency about the work. The Ixil people are responding and I want to be a part of this special moment in their history."

Paul said good night and I thanked him for his willingness to share part of his remarkable story. As he left I thought to myself, now here is a person like my flinty friend in Ecuador who lived out his faith in practical reality. Paul has willingly faced misunderstanding and come into conflict with the status-quo in order to take seriously Christ's command to love one's neighbor as himself.

I close this book with one other statement by Paul Townsend that clarifies my assignment, and hopefully yours as co-laborers in the overall work of Bible translation:

One thing that has impressed me is the need to work together more as a body. We need our supporters and prayer partners and we need colleagues with a variety of talents and temperaments. My strong points are not your strong points and vice versa. Therefore, we truly do need to combine our talents and gifts and work together for the glory of God.

NOTES

[1] J.B. Phillips, *The Newborn Christian* (New York: MacMillan Publishing Co., 1984), p.114. Used by permission.

[2] Hugh Steven, *They Dared to be Different* (1976; reprint, Huntington Beach: Wycliffe Bible Translators, Inc., 1983).

[3] Phillips, *The Newborn Christian*.

[4] Hugh Steven, *To the Ends of the Earth* (Chappaqua: Christian Herald Books, 1978).

[5] Eric Fromm, *The Art of Loving* (New York: Harper and Row, Inc., 1956).

[6] Hugh Steven, *Manuel*, 2nd ed. (Huntington Beach: Wycliffe Bible Translators, Inc., 1970).

[7] Cornell Capa and Dale Kietzman, eds., *Language and Faith* (Santa Ana: Wycliffe Bible Translators, Inc., 1972).

[8] Hugh Steven, *It Takes Time to Love* (Huntington Beach: Wycliffe Bible Translators, Inc., 1974).

[9] Hugh Steven, *Man With the Noisy Heart* (Chicago: Moody Press, 1979).

[10] James C. Hefley, *Peril by Choice* (Grand Rapids: Zondervan Publishing House, 1968).

[11] John Beekman and John Callow, *Translating the Word of God* (Grand Rapids: Zondervan Publishing House, 1960).

[12]Hugh Steven, *Man With the Noisy Heart*.

[13]Beekman and Callow, *Translating the Word of God*.

[14]Wycliffe Bible Translators, Inc., comp., *Pass the Word* (Huntington Beach: Wycliffe Bible Translators, Inc., 1984).

[15]C.S. Lewis, *Mere Christianity* (New York: Macmillan Publishing Co., Inc., 1960).

[16]Hugh Steven, *A Thousand Trails* (Langley, B.C., Canada: CREDO Publishing Corporation, 1984).

For more information regarding Hugh Steven's books write to:

> Book Room
> Wycliffe Bible Translators, Inc.
> Huntington Beach, CA 92647

All author royalties received from the sale of Hugh Steven's books go directly to Wycliffe Bible Translators, Inc.

To return evil for evil, or wound for wound, is a cultural norm for many of Irian Jaya's ethnic groups.

"The New Authority" in Mariano's life effects a change in an American businessman's life.

A grandmother with deep, weathered lines etched into her bronzed face is lost in a sea of memories.

The "Bridge of Pain" was a long-forgotten memory on the day Ken and Elaine Jacobs addressed the Chamula believers on the occasion of their first baptismal service.

Dr. Burt Bascom explains a reading chart prior to the sale of the Tepehuan New Testament.

Narcisa, co-translator of the Tepehuan New Testament, radiates her joy over its completion.

Lulu Reber shows her true character as one who has taken the place of a willing servant even to washing out a pair of muddy tennis shoes.

These two Chinatec believers, two of the very first to "grab hold of the Word of God," exemplify J.B. Phillips words, ". . . in the young Church there was joy and indomitable hope."

Jerry Ferguson, a skilled JAARS pilot, relies on his compass readings and God's grace to guide him over Irian Jaya's uncharted rain forest.

Author Hugh Steven on a story assignment, strapped into a three-seater Hiller helicopter in Irian Jaya.

Neil Anderson interacts with a group of Podopa believers who are learning to assume the responsibility for Bible translation.

Don Hesse Photo

Author Hugh Steven "behind the story" (and almost in the river) in Sabah, Malaysia.
Carolyn Miller Photo

Martha King oversees the Cakchiquel Multi-Translation Project and checks a calendar for accuracy with a Cakchiquel colleague.

Cakchiquel workers on the CMTP discuss the translation in one of six Cakchiquel dialects.

Paul Townsend encouraging a group of Ixil children to become literate in their own language.   *Paul Townsend Photo*

Ixil Christians reach out beyond their cultural patterns to help those who can't help themselves. In this case, volunteer workers built houses for widows whose husbands were killed in Guatemala's political conflict.   *Paul Townsend Photo*